Mad and Dad

Mad and Bad

Real Heroines of the Regency

Bea Koch

GRAND CENTRAL
PUBLISHING

NEW YORK BOSTON

Grand Central Publishing
Hachette Book Group
1290 Avenue of the Americas, New York, NY 10104
grandcentralpublishing.com
twitter.com/grandcentralpub

First Edition: September 2020

Grand Central Publishing is a division of Hachette Book Group, Inc. The Grand Central Publishing name and logo is a trademark of Hachette Book Group, Inc.

Chapter and part opener illustrations by Jay Bradley, Sacred Studios.

Library of Congress Cataloging-in-Publication Data
Names: Koch, Bea, author.
Title: Mad and Bad : Real Heroines of the Regency / Bea Koch.
Description: First edition. | New York : Grand Central Publishing, 2020. | Includes bibliographical references and index. | Summary: "A feminist pop history that looks beyond the Ton and Jane Austen to highlight iconoclastic women of the Regency period who succeeded on their own terms and have largely been lost to history"—Provided by publisher.
Identifiers: LCCN 2019049246 | ISBN 9781538701010 (trade paperback) | ISBN 9781538701027 (ebook)
Subjects: LCSH: Women—Great Britain—19th century—Biography. | Women—Great Britain—Intellectual life—19th century. | Women intellectuals—Great Britain—Biography. | England—Social life and customs—19th century. | Great Britain—History—George IV, 1820-1830—Biography.
Classification: LCC HQ1595.A3 K64 220 | DDC 305.4092/241 [B]—dc23
LC record available at https://lccn.loc.gov/2019049246

ISBNs: 978-1-5387-0101-0 (trade pbk.), 978-1-5387-0102-7 (ebook)

Printed in the United States of America

LSC-C

10 9 8 7 6 5 4 3 2 1

For

My mom, my first editor

My dad, my compass in everything

Leah, Jacob, Olivia, and Mo, my people

and Blake, my future

Contents

Mad and Bad

Introduction to the Regency World and Why We're Here

"Mad, bad, and dangerous to know."[1]

Caroline Lamb claimed credit for those words, the most famous description of Lord George Byron, poet and all-around bad boy of early-nineteenth-century England.

She might as well have been describing herself. Caroline was equally as dramatic, talented, capricious, and fascinating as Byron. And just like Byron, she was a published author.

But Byron is remembered as a great writer of the era, while

Caroline's writing has become a footnote, and she is relegated to the role of hysterical ex-girlfriend in Byron's story.

To many the Regency is a period of great men. Castlereagh, Palmerston, Pitt, Nelson, Wellington dominate the histories of the era; their names writ large across the historical stage.

But it is also an era of great women. Forcing their way into a historical record set up to extol the many accomplishments of men in so many surprising places that we are forced to take notice.

Each woman shines bright, illuminating those around her. Each woman connects to so many more.

Each has her own story. Her own accomplishments and disappointments. Her own love stories and losses.

The sad truth of history is that so many of these stories are lost. And the stories of people of color and women are disproportionately so.

The happy truth is that we're still rediscovering stories every day. History is more alive than ever as we turn our attention to those who have been left to languish in the shadows and those who have been cast in a singular light.

Here we have an opportunity to examine these networks of women spreading through an iconic time period: the Regency.

So named for the ten-year period between 1810 and 1820 when then Prince of Wales George IV became Regent after his father, George III, showed increasing signs of mental instability, "the Regency" has long reigned supreme in the beloved world of historical romances. These romance novels have helped the Regency become what it is—and all that it means—today.

There has long been a misperception that Regency romance heroines are simpering misses who fall fast for a rake and think of nothing but love and, more crudely, sex. In actuality, contemporary romance novelists have always plumbed the depths of Regency history to find inspiration for heroines who break the mold, in more ways than one.

Lady Caroline Lamb is a perfect example of one such Regency woman, one who lived the type of life that could inspire a slew of romance novels. Her love life was certainly dramatic enough. But there is another layer to the story, a twin narrative that follows the more famous love affair and that peeks out at us in letters, diaries, and poems.

It's the network of women in Caroline's life who loved her and she loved back. And the women she sparred with in person and letters, those she tried desperately to befriend and those she scorned. Mother, grandmothers, aunts, sisters, cousins, friends, enemies, and in-laws: They appear in every facet of Caroline's life, guiding and worrying over her, cajoling and encouraging, censorious and generous, or in turn demanding and threatening as they tried to force Caroline to live as they wanted her to. It is an altogether familiar world for modern women—one that the women in our lives create through their very presence. Caroline lived in a world of women, even if she is historically associated with famous men.

There is such joy and strength in female friendship, and it is that joy that we can see in every facet of women's lives during the Regency—and similarly that joy and connection that are all too frequently left out of the greater historical narrative.

It is touching to see echoes of that care and closeness we crave today in historical sources, like the famous Duchess of Devonshire's sweet poem to her niece, the eventual Lady Caroline Lamb, née Ponsonby.

To Lady Caroline Ponsonby With a
New Year's gift of a pencil:

Fairy, sprite, whatever thou art
Magic genius waits on thee
And thou claimst each willing heart
Whilst thy airy form we see

Take the gift, the early year
Shall for thee in Splendor shine.
Genius gives it. Do not fear
Boldly mould, invent, design.[2]

Georgiana and Caroline are both famous for their scandalous love lives and social antics. But in this poem all that melts away, and we see something far more intimate and honest. It echoes through time, reminding each new generation of the gift that can come when someone sees you and believes in you. And it reminds us of the humanity that we sometimes forget in the greater historical narrative.

The bittersweet nature of these relationships can also be seen in Caroline's constant push-and-pull with her in-laws and friends who turned critics as her antics came right up to the edge, and eventually over it, of socially acceptable.

Caroline has been called shameless and hysterical for her refusal to go quietly into the night when Byron was done with her. In actuality, her struggle to wrest control of her story from all those who would misrepresent her is familiar to the women of the twenty-first century. In her rejection of social norms and polite society we see glimmers of Elizabeth Warren's famous "Nevertheless, she persisted" attitude.

And like our heroines of the twenty-first century, Caroline was a complicated woman who made mistakes. In that, she had many contemporary examples, including her own aunt, Georgiana.

The famous Duchess of Devonshire died in 1806, before her friend George IV officially became Prince Regent. But Georgiana's fingerprints can be seen all over the Regency. She was a friend and, more important, patron of any number of the women in this book. Indeed, the famous portrait commemorating her friendship with Anne Damer and Elizabeth, Lady Melbourne, stares at us from the pages of this book.

Elizabeth, Lady Melbourne, was also Lady Caroline Lamb's mother-in-law.

Connections everywhere, binding disparate women into remarkable networks.

In choosing the women to feature in this book I was faced with an interesting dilemma in considering who was truly a heroine of the *Regency* and what that meant. I have focused on women who contributed to the culture of a time period, which means, necessarily, that there are women featured who were prominent before and after this ten-year period. I would argue, strongly, that if we discount those who come immediately before and after, we lose something essential in our understanding of women at this time.

Indeed, we lose the very essence of what is so remarkable about the women of the nineteenth century—the connections they created through friendship, family, talent, and intellect, and the way they fostered their own ambitions and those of other women through careful patronage and targeted support.

The Regency era of our imagination isn't simply ten years. It's actually a much broader period, blending with the Georgian and Victorian on either end. And the truth is that there are hundreds of women who could be included in these pages.

I'm often asked why the Regency is so perennially popular. What exactly about this tiny time period grabs and holds our attention?

I would argue that one part of the fascination is in the struggle of a society seemingly ruled by a strict social code while in actuality the most famous and celebrated of the time are those who flouted those rules.

And no one more so than the women in this book. They lived life on their own terms and made the rules bend to accommodate them. They built careers in the most improbable places and demanded respect for their accomplishments.

The real heroines of the Regency aren't empty-headed heiresses or scheming mamas—they're intelligent, talented artists, thinkers, scientists, and so much more.

CHAPTER ONE

The Ton

Either You're In or You're Out

It is a truth universally acknowledged, that a single man in possession of a good fortune, must be in want of a wife.

—Jane Austen, *Pride and Prejudice*, 1813

Marriage now is a necessary kind of barter, and an alliance of families; —the heart is not consulted; —or, if that should

> sometimes bring a pair together, —judgement being left far behind, love seldom lasts long.
>
> —Georgiana, Duchess of Devonshire, *The Sylph*, 1779

The first line of *Pride and Prejudice*—*the* defining novel of the Regency era by Jane Austen—tells us everything we need to know about the focus and priorities of the upper classes.[1] Marriage, and in particular the right marriage, ensured that the wealth concentrated among a few families remained exactly where they wanted it, passed down through the generations, consolidating and consecrating their power. This singular obsession runs through sources from the time both consciously and less obviously so.

The discussion of marriage and what it truly means is put into even more material terms in Georgiana, Duchess of Devonshire's novel *The Sylph*, but it's no less harsh a description of the institution and the way her entire social circle treated it during the time period.

Both Georgiana and Jane highlight the mercantile reality of marriage for the upper classes. Money needs to marry. And during the Regency, these marriages were plotted and encouraged during social events held over a social Season, like the Wednesday-evening ball held weekly at Almack's Assembly Rooms.

The Assembly Rooms and the "marriage mart" culture they encouraged have been immortalized in the fictional worlds of Jane and Georgiana and their fellow nineteenth-century authors, which in turn captured the imaginations of historical romance novelists, who frequently feature Almack's and the marriage machinations taking place therein in their Regency-set romances.

Almack's and the Patronesses who ran the membership lists for the club, deciding who was awarded a voucher for entry and who was denied, have become a beloved and expected part of a Regency romance novel. The Patronesses are often portrayed as middle-aged and meddling (if invariably with a well-hidden streak of kindness), ruling their club with an iron fist and eye to the unwritten set of rules that governed the world of the aristocracy.

In reality the Patronesses were young women themselves, many of them friends or related through marriage, who lived the kind of interesting, exciting lives that Regency romance heroines aspire to.

ALMACK'S: A BRIEF HISTORY

Almack's Assembly Rooms were founded around 1765 by William Almack, who originally had a coffeehouse and tavern on the premises.[2] By the height of the Regency his daughter Elizabeth Pitcairn had inherited and was running her father's establishment. The coffeehouse and tavern had morphed into a much more elegant operation, with a series of large ballrooms connected to one another.

Almack's was one of the first clubs in London to admit both men and women. Men's clubs were already very popular with upper-class men as a space for socializing. Almack's allowed women into this inner sanctum.

Even more uniquely, the list of those admitted was ruled over by a group of aristocratic women, called the Patronesses.

The Patronesses were an integral part of William Almack's vision for his club. He wanted to ensure an elite reputation for his establishment, and knew that engaging the services of the most aristocratic women he could find would help achieve this goal. In his original advertisement for Almack's he announced that seven aristocratic women had each opened a subscription book with the intention of giving sixty subscriptions apiece, which would confer the right to the holder to pay ten guineas for admission to the twelve balls a Season.

In doing so he created a uniquely feminine space where aristocratic men and women could meet and continue the conversations that had been occurring in Parliament and elsewhere, with an eye to keeping their social world rigorously regulated through careful, often arranged marriages and courtships. But unlike Parliament, women ruled at Almack's.

Almack's and its Patronesses truly capture the many contradictions of Regency society. Even during their lifetime, they were characters of fascination and subjected to satirical representations as well as public gossip about their lives. The Patronesses were never neutral figures. By entering a world of power and setting themselves up as the ones to control it, the Patronesses found themselves in an unusual position. They wielded authority over those who traditionally never gave up power to anyone.

The Regency-era Patronesses of Almack's are often remembered and associated with a number of incidents that occurred during their tenure, perhaps none more famous than Wellington and his trousers.

Almack's was governed by a strict set of rules, which included a dress code. In May 1819 the Duke of Wellington arrived at Almack's with the necessary voucher to attend the ball. However, he was turned away at the door because he was wearing full-length trousers, rather than the required knee-breeches. The Patronesses' rejection of the new fashion reminds us of their core of conservativeness. Another rumor goes that he was turned away for arriving seven minutes after the doors had closed, necessitating the steward to ask the Patronesses to hold the door for him, a request that was refused.

Wellington was a lionized and beloved figure in the press and with the people for defeating Napoleon in the Battle of Waterloo. The Patronesses were painted as ridiculous and petty to deny entrance to such a figure due to a simple fashion error. Rather than being considered fair, they were seen as small, mean, and so obsessed with their own rules that they couldn't bend them, even for such a great hero.

The sheer uncomfortableness of Regency men with this exceptional display of feminine power can be seen in the contemporary writing about Almack's, like Henry Luttrell's *Advice to Julia*, which features the lines:

All on that magic List depends;
Fame, fortune, fashion, lovers, friends;
'Tis that which gratifies or vexes
All ranks, all ages, and both sexes.
If once to Almack's you belong,
Like monarchs you can do no wrong;
But banished thence on Wednesday night,
By Jove, you can do nothing right.[3]

Luttrell bemoans the fact that the Patronesses have circumvented traditional power structures, and have specifically rejected the traits that would normally ensure social acceptance. Instead they have created their own "list," and only they know the secret formula for guaranteeing a name's inclusion.

Contemporary (and slightly later) chroniclers of the time have been less than kind to the Patronesses, perhaps no one more so than Rees Howell Gronow, known as Captain Gronow.

A Welsh officer in the Welsh Grenadier Guards, Gronow arrived in London in 1813 after serving with his regiment in Spain. He was a popular society figure, attending Almack's Wednesday-night balls along with his fellow dandies. His military career continued and took him to Paris. He retired and struggled financially, while attempting to mount a political career—which failed. In 1862 he published the first of what would eventually be four volumes of *Reminiscences*, his true legacy.

Captain Gronow had a lot of opinions, some of them worthy of a great deal of skepticism, and he shared them freely. In 1813 he recorded the Patronesses as: Sarah Villiers, the Countess of Jersey; Emily Clavering-Cowper (later Viscountess Palmerston); Dorothea, Princess Lieven; Clementina Drummond-Burrell; Amelia, Viscountess Castlereagh; Maria, Viscountess Sefton; and Princess Esterhazy.

According to Captain Gronow, Sarah Villiers, Lady Jersey, was a "theatrical tragedy queen" and "inconceivably rude," in contrast with Emily Clavering-Cowper, later Viscountess Palmerston, whom he names as the most popular of the Patronesses.

To Captain Gronow, Princess Lieven is "haughty and exclusive" and Lady Castlereagh and Mrs. Drummond-Burrell are the "grand dames" of the proceedings. Meanwhile, Lady Sefton is described as "kind and amiable" while Princess Esterhazy is given the nickname of "bon Enfant," which can mean both "good-natured" and, in a less charitable reading, "simple-minded and naive."[4]

Gronow's descriptions might often be unkind, but they hint at the differences among the Patronesses. We often think of this group of women as a unit, but they were individuals with different lives and ambitions. We also see these descriptors pop up again and again in almost any future mention of the Patronesses either together or separately, highlighting the way fact and fiction can become entwined in a historical source.

But what is even more interesting is to examine what the Patronesses thought of one another, and their impressions of each other.

Princess Lieven is a wonderful source for this. A prodigious letter writer separated from her family due to her husband's ambassadorship in London, Princess Lieven wrote thousands of letters to her family and friends, keeping them abreast of everything happening in Regency England, and Lieven's opinions on it all.

Princess Lieven describes Princess Esterhazy as "small, round, black, animated, and somewhat spiteful,"[5] which is oft referenced when discussing the two women. However, Princess Lieven is not only discussing Princess Esterhazy, but also comparing her with another recently arrived ambassador's wife, and after her description of the pair, she writes, "I get on equally well with both."[6]

The princesses are often compared to one another as the only two foreign-born Patronesses, with Princess Lieven cast as the jealous older woman worried about losing her position of power to the younger, prettier Princess Esterhazy. But the princess's letters reveal something far more interesting: two power players jockeying for favor and position in the world they both entered as foreigners.

Princess Lieven mentions her fellow Patronesses regularly in her gossipy letters, sometimes hinting at historical intrigues long forgotten, as in her discussion of her fellow Patroness Clementina Burrell-Drummond, who seems to have been kicked out of the Prince Regent's inner circle due to her friendship with an out-of-favor mistress, only to be brought back into the fold when he became king.[7]

The Patronesses were larger than life. But in studying the details of those lives we can see that in actuality, the women who held themselves up as moral authorities were often the most scandalous of all, or at the very least intimately connected to the scandalous ones.

Part of the fascination with the Regency seems to come from exactly this touchpoint of the rules of a society and what happened to those who flouted them. The Patronesses were not the only aristocratic women to skirt this line between respectable and scandalous, but they were also the ones in the unique position of casting judgment upon their fellow aristocrats.

Rules are, of course, made to be broken.

THE PATRONESSES

Sarah Villiers, Countess of Jersey

Born: Sarah Sophia Child Fane

Married name: Sarah Sophia Child Villiers, Countess of Jersey

Notable lovers: Henry Temple, Viscount Palmerston

Nickname: "Silence"

Sarah Sophia Child Villiers, née Fane, Countess of Jersey, is perhaps the most often mentioned and best remembered of the Patronesses, immortalized in her contemporary Lady Caroline Lamb's novel *Glenarvon* as Lady Augusta and by later writer Georgette Heyer as "Queen of London's most exclusive club."[8]

She was born March 4, 1785, to John Fane, tenth Earl of Westmoreland, and Sarah Anne Child. Her mother, Sarah Anne, was the daughter of Sarah Jodrell and Robert Child, a banker and politician.

John and Sarah Anne eloped to Gretna Green in 1782, against Robert Child's express wishes. He did not approve of his daughter's husband and arranged for his fortune to pass to his daughter, and then her children, effectively writing the earl out of his inheritance.

It worked. Sarah Anne's daughter Sarah inherited the family estate Osterley Park and also became a principal shareholder in the family banking firm, Child & Co. Sarah's husband, George Villiers, fifth Earl of Jersey, had the surname Child added to his own by royal license, fulfilling a long-held family wish.

Sarah married George in 1804. The marriage, like those of so many of their contemporaries, was not a faithful one. Despite Sarah's determination to stand in contrast to her notorious mother-in-law, Frances Villiers, who was famously mistress to George IV while he was Prince Regent (the prince had a thing for older women), she was not a faithful wife. One of her most famous supposed lovers was Henry

Temple, Viscount Palmerston, who would go on to marry Sarah's fellow Patroness, Emily Clavering-Cowper.

Sarah was a complicated figure. She was immortalized in many contemporary pieces of fiction, sometimes in a less-than-flattering light. In fiction Sarah is alternately meddling and severe, but in real life, Regency chronicler E. Beresford Chancellor wrote that "her amiable manners, her interest in politics, her admirable linguistic powers, her kindly, genial nature, all combined to give her a sort of prescriptive right to the exalted sphere in which she moved."[9] Sarah's fellow Patroness Princess Lieven wrote that Sarah was the only other society hostess who threw as elegant a party as she did, and she mentioned Sarah many times in her letters as a friend.

Sarah had seven children, who all went on to make the kind of socially advantageous marriages Almack's was supposed to facilitate. But perhaps most neatly for us, her daughter Lady Sarah Frederica Caroline Child Villiers married Nicholas Paul, ninth Prince Esterhazy and son of Lady Jersey's fellow Patroness Princess Esterhazy, uniting the two families.

Sarah is also remembered for introducing the quadrille to Almack's in 1816. [Figure 1] Up until that point, only country dances had been allowed at the Wednesday-night balls. This, along with the fact that only light refreshments were served, contributed to a stuffy reputation for Almack's. Quadrilles are performed by four couples, arranged in a square set. In the early nineteenth century they were complicated dances that required the dancers to memorize a series of elaborate sets. While country dances were inclusive and easier for anyone to join, quadrilles could only be danced by those "in the know." Perfect for members of a social club looking to make themselves even more exclusive!

Sarah Villiers, Countess of Jersey, Queen of the Ton, was the daughter of a banker and an heiress to boot. These are two qualities that fiction has told us would have resulted in her exclusion from the very exalted circles she ran. Instead she ruled over a legendary social scene, turning the tables on the Ton and holding court from her position of power as both a Patroness and a partner at Child & Co. Sarah never relinquished control of the bank to any of the men in her life, retaining the right to hire and fire partners and attending meetings regularly herself.

Sarah's nickname was, ironically, Silence, due to her supposed penchant for rambling storytelling. But in Sarah we see a woman who refused to be quiet about the things that mattered to her, and instead used her considerable wealth, power, and personal charm to achieve her goals. Henry Greville, third Earl of Warwick, wrote about Sarah in his diary, "Few women have played a more brilliant part in society, or have commanded more homage, than Lady Jersey... It was her great zest and gaiety, rather than her cleverness, which constituted her power of attracting remarkable men, many of whom I have seen listen with the greatest complacency to what they would have considered to be egregious nonsense had it emanated from less charming lips."[10] And then, attesting to the true legacy Sarah left behind, "She will be a great loss to many, and she is the last, with the exception of Lady Palmerston, of a more brilliant and more refined society than is to be found in our present time."[11]

Emily Temple, Viscountess Palmerston

Born: The Honorable Emily Lamb

Married name: First, Emily Clavering-Cowper, Countess Cowper; second, Emily Temple, Viscountess Palmerston

Notable lovers: Diplomat Carlo Andrea Pozzo di Borgo and Henry Temple, Viscount Palmerston

Emily had many names throughout her life. She was born Emily Lamb in 1787, but even her birth surname was in question as her mother, Elizabeth, was famously unfaithful to her husband Peniston Lamb, bringing Emily's parentage into question. Peniston was made Viscount Melbourne in 1781, honoring the family's contributions to politics and changing Emily's title for the first time, as she became the Honorable Emily Lamb.

Emily's glamorous mother, Elizabeth Lamb, Viscountess Melbourne, can be seen alongside Georgiana, Duchess of Devonshire, and Anne Damer in the famous Macbeth witches portrait by Daniel Gardner. [Figure 14] Elizabeth's many affairs distressed her children, but she remained a fierce advocate for her offspring, working hard to ensure successful marriages for all of them.

In 1805 eighteen-year-old Emily married Peter Clavering-Cowper, fifth Earl of Cowper. The two were wildly different, with the charming, vivacious Emily often outshining her more quiet and reserved husband. The couple had five children, though the paternity of two of them is in question. Their marriage was not a faithful one, but Emily's most famous affair led to an even rarer thing: a happy second marriage with her former paramour Henry John Temple, third Viscount Palmerston. Palmerston earned the nickname Cupid for his many affairs, including with two of Emily's fellow Patronesses, Princess Lieven and Lady Jersey.

From her deathbed Emily's mother, Elizabeth, urged Emily to remain faithful to Palmerston, her lover, rather than her husband.

Peter Clavering-Cowper died in 1837, two days into the reign of Queen Victoria, leaving Emily free to marry Palmerston. However, the pair first had to secure the new queen's blessing, which they did.

Emily and Palmerston married in 1839. Emily was fifty-two, and her new husband was fifty-five. Even their contemporaries were in awe of the seeming happiness of the new couple. Emily's son-in-law Lord Shaftesbury wrote about his in-laws, "His attentions to Lady Palmerston, when they both of them were well stricken in years, were those of a perpetual courtship. The sentiment was reciprocal; and I have frequently seen them go out on a morning to plant some trees, almost believing that they would live to eat the fruit, or sit together under the shade."[12]

Palmerston died in 1865 and Emily died four years later. She is remembered as the kindest and most generous of the Almack's Patronesses, especially for her role in her sister-in-law Lady Caroline Lamb's banishment from Almack's. Despite her difficult relationship with Caroline, Emily went out of her way to convince Lady Jersey to rescind the ban and allow her to return. This may have been partly for Emily's brother William's benefit. But the close family ties and complicated loyalties only highlight the small circles in which the Patronesses lived and loved. And serve to humanize Emily. In the world of Almack's, Emily is a kind and generous cipher. But in private letters about her sister-in-law, we can see a fuller being, one who loses the sheen that history has put on her.

While the strict code ruling Almack's was enforced when those outside the inner circle transgressed, strings could always be pulled, depending on who you knew. The Patronesses were only human, and therefore very fallible. Emily's story can sometimes be overshadowed by her more dramatic friends and family, and her true impact can be lost in her own love affairs. But in her letters we can see the important role Emily played in the lives of her many friends, family, and lovers. And what a collection they are! Emily was related to or friendly with so many of the movers and shakers of the Regency, political, artistic, and more. As a Patroness she carved a place of power for herself and was not shy about using said power for herself, her family, and her friends. Her five children all made socially impressive marriages, and her brother William Lamb, Viscount Melbourne, became prime minister of England, an appointment Emily actively campaigned for.

Katharina Alexandra Dorothea Fürstin von Lieven

Born: Katharina Alexandra Dorothea Freiin von Benckendorff

Married name: Katharina Alexandra Dorothea Fürstin von Lieven

Notable lovers: Austrian foreign minister Klemens von Metternich, François Guizot, George IV

Katharina Alexandra Dorothea Freiin von Benckendorff was born into Russian royalty on December 17, 1785. Her father,

General Baron Christoph von Benckendorff, was the military governor of Livonia, and his wife, Baroness Anna Juliane Charlotte Schilling von Canstatt, was a senior lady-in-waiting and best friend to Empress Maria Feodorovna.

Known as Dorothea, she was sent to the exclusive Smolny Convent Institute in St. Petersburg to be educated. Her brothers Alexander and Konstantin were Russian generals whom she stayed close to even as life brought them far apart. Her letters to Alexander in particular are some of the best, most gossipy sources on the period.

At just fourteen she was married to General Count Christoph von Lieven. Christoph was a working diplomat and in 1812 was appointed ambassador to Great Britain. In England, Dorothea shined as a political and social hostess. She was so popular that she was elected the first foreign-born Patroness of Almack's.

Like her fellow Patronesses, Dorothea carried on several high-profile affairs with a who's who of the political world, including the Austrian foreign minister Klemens von Metternich. She also served as an ambassador in her own right, carrying out a secret mission for Tsar Alexander I that led to the Protocol of St. Petersburg.

In October 1825 the tsar took advantage of Dorothea's popularity and importance in English society, sending her to the fashionable seaside resort Brighton for an off-the-record meeting with the British foreign secretary George Canning. There she delivered a message from the tsar: He wanted Russia and England to intervene in the Greek War of Independence, noting the planned persecution and deportation of Greek Christians by the Ottoman Empire.

This conversation led to the Anglo-Russian agreement known

as the Protocol of St. Petersburg, where the countries agreed to intervene in the war and negotiate its end.

In 1834 diplomatic relations between Russia and England became so bad that the Lievens were recalled to Russia. The British press reacted to this news with glee. *The Times* wrote, "There never figured on the Courtly stage a female intriguer more restless, more arrogant, more mischievous, more (politically, and therefore we mean it not offensively) odious and insufferable than this supercilious Ambassadress. She fancied herself 'a power.' She was, however, more frequently a dupe, the dupe of her own artifices reacted upon by those of others."[13]

Regardless of the mockery by the press, Dorothea was reluctant to leave England after twenty-plus years living there. But she dutifully followed her husband to Russia, where their two young sons succumbed to scarlet fever and died. That was the last straw for the Lievens' marriage.

Unhappy with her life, Dorothea made a move completely familiar to a twenty-first-century woman and completely baffling in the context of the nineteenth century, leaving the protection and privilege her marriage afforded her. Against her husband's wishes she left Russia and settled in Paris. There she hosted a popular salon and finally openly enjoyed the political power that she deserved. Continuing her tradition of attaching herself to brilliant, powerful men, she started a relationship with François Guizot, a French statesman, in 1837.

Dorothea fled the revolution and France in 1848, settling in Brighton where she reunited with an old lover, the recently resigned Austrian foreign minister Klemens von Metternich. Their reconciliation was arranged by Metternich's third wife, Countess

Melanie Zichy-Ferraris, apparently unthreatened by the couple's hours spent reminiscing about old times.

Dorothea returned to Paris in time to meet Napoleon Louis's proposed bride, Eugénie de Montijo.

She died in Paris in 1857 with François Guizot and one of her surviving sons at her deathbed.

Count Joseph Alexander Hübner, an Austrian diplomat living in Paris, wrote upon her death, "Last night one of the personalities who, for half a century, ranked as the most notable in the diplomatic world and on the great European scene, disappeared from it."[14]

The Patronesses can be confined to the ballrooms of Almack's by history, but Dorothea's life shows us just how far outside London their influence could be felt.

Clementina Drummond-Burrell

Born: Sarah Clementina Drummond

Married name: Sarah Clementina Drummond-Burrell

Clementina is often overlooked among the flashier Patronesses. Born in Edinburgh on May 5, 1786, to James Perth, Lord Perth, Baron Drummond of Stobhall, and the Honorable Clementina Elphinstone, Clementina was the only surviving child and heir. When her father died in 1800, she inherited a considerable estate and fortune.

In 1807 Clementina married the Honorable Peter Burrell. The couple took the name Drummond-Burrell by royal decree, ensuring that Clementina's father's name would continue.

Peter Drummond-Burrell is remembered as a dandy, but unlike her fellow Patronesses, Clementina kept her name free of scandalous associations. After his parents' deaths, Peter inherited their titles and the couple became known as Lord and Lady Willoughby de Eresby. They had five children. Clementina died in 1865, and her husband followed a short month later.

Georgette Heyer included Clementina in her Regency romance novel *Friday's Child* (1944), where she calls her "the most coldly correct of the Almack's patronesses."[15] Captain Gronow called her a "très grande dame" in his *Reminiscences*.[16] She's frequently referred to by historians as a "stickler," but Princess Lieven remembers her fondly in her letters, writing that Clementina is a great "resource" to her and a dear friend she looks forward to seeing.[17] Lieven also recounts Clementina falling in and out of favor with the Prince Regent, due to a friendship with one of his many mistresses, possibly Lady Hertford. This drama is mentioned in contemporary letters in passing, with little attention to the specific details of this particular episode, reminding us of the fleeting nature of royal favor and that even the Patronesses needed to tread lightly around the Prince Regent.

And it adds another facet of fun to Clementina's rigid historical reputation. Much like her fellow Patroness Sarah Villiers, Lady Jersey, Clementina was a banking heiress. And much like Sarah, Clementina has a reputation that seems set in stone. But Clementina was only twenty-eight years old when she served as an Almack's Patroness, far from the middle-aged stickler who scares all of Georgette Heyer's heroines. She has a number of Scottish reels (dances) named after her. And there are stories of raucous parties thrown at her home.

In reducing any of the Patronesses to their most baseline descriptors, we do a disservice to this vibrant and varied group of women. Each lived such a full, fascinating life. And their mark on the period is truly indelible, even if they're only remembered as a "Patroness."

Amelia Stewart, Viscountess of Castlereagh

Born: Amelia Anne "Emily" Hobart

Married name: Amelia Anne "Emily" Stewart, Viscountess of Castlereagh and Marchioness of Londonderry

Amelia Anne Hobart, known as Emily, was born on February 20, 1772, to John Hobart, second Earl of Buckinghamshire, and Caroline Conolly. Her father was a diplomat who served as ambassador to Russia and lord lieutenant of Ireland. Her mother was from one of the wealthiest families in Ireland.

In 1794 Emily married Robert Stewart, Viscount Castlereagh, until he succeeded to the marquessate upon his father's death in 1821.

Emily and Castlereagh settled in London but traveled together often, with Emily serving as a social hostess in support of her husband's career. Castlereagh served as British foreign secretary from 1812 until 1822. He was a key member of the British government's efforts to defeat Napoleon, and he represented the country at the Congress of Vienna.

Castlereagh was known for his cold demeanor, a reputation encouraged by the poet Percy Shelley, who included Castlereagh as a mask worn by Murder in his political poem *The Masque of Anarchy* (1819). But his personal letters to his wife show a very different side.

> I cannot go to bed without telling you, dearest Emily, that I am really emancipated, I do it in the full confidence that you will read it with a sensation not less animated and satisfactory than that with which it is written. I don't know what you feel, but I am quite determined, unless you differ, never to pass from one country to another, even for a day, without you. You know how little I am given to professions, but I have really of late felt ye deprivation with an acuteness which is only known to those who are separated from what they most love. But I find I am in danger of committing the intolerable barbarism of writing a love letter to my wife.[18]

Castlereagh was under immense pressure for his entire career, which spanned a time of enormous global change. In 1822, while serving as Leader of the House of Commons, Castlereagh began to suffer from paranoia. He became convinced that he was going to be accused of being a homosexual. In a meeting with the king on August 9 he referred to the recent case of the Bishop of Clogher, who was forced from his position due to similar accusations. On August 12 Castlereagh found a small knife (his wife had hid his razor) and slit his own throat.

Castlereagh's suicide is a complicated issue for historians, made even more difficult by the contemporary reaction to the tragic death, which saw many of Castlereagh's friends blaming Emily for concealing the true extent of her husband's mental health problems until it was too late. In reality it seems Emily might not have known how serious it was. Without many choices she trusted her husband's doctor. Despite, or perhaps because of, all her wealth and connections, Emily could not protect her husband from himself.

After her husband's death, Emily retired to their country home Woollett Hall, where she famously kept a zoo. She collected animals from all over the world, some sent by enterprising diplomats hoping to gain favor with her husband. This eccentricity added to the overall dismissal of Emily as a lightweight, especially in comparison with her brilliant husband.

Emily spent two years in seclusion, mourning the death of her husband, before she returned to society. Her contemporaries were particularly censorious about this decision, painting it as cold and unfeeling, but it was fully within keeping with the standards of the time. Regency mourning rituals were not as rigid as during the later Victorian period, but still important. Wives were expected to spend twelve months mourning a lost spouse, during which they were expected to wear black and receive only family visitors and close friends.

Emily died in 1829, seven years after her husband.

In comparison with her brilliant and troubled spouse, Emily has been cast as the frivolous wife, more concerned with her duties as an Almack's Patroness and her dogs than serious political matters. But this picture misses the vital way she contributed to and furthered his career, supporting and advocating for Castlereagh in the very feminine but no less important social sphere.

In 1814 Castlereagh attended the Congress of Vienna as Britain's foreign secretary and the architect of their proposal for a system in which members met regularly and in return provided safety and security collectively. Emily was by his side, visibly enough that it was noted by his fellow diplomats.

WHAT'S THE POINT OF PATRONAGE?

In 1935 Georgette Heyer published her first Regency romance novel, *Regency Buck*. With it, she helped to establish a new subgenre of romance, one that is still popular to this day. Heyer did immense amounts of meticulous research for her novels, including many historical facts and figures in her stories about young women falling in love and finding happy endings in early-nineteenth-century England.

The Lady Patronesses of Almack's are common figures in Heyer's Regency world.

Heyer's heroines vie for approval from the Patronesses, hoping to win the all-important voucher to secure their place at the most important balls of the Season.

The titular character in *Frederica* quickly reveals that it is her dearest wish that her beautiful younger sister Charis receive a voucher for Almack's, a dream that her distant relative and soon-to-be love interest the Marquis of Alverstoke initially laughs at. Eventually Alverstoke finagles them an invitation from Lady Jersey and they all live happily ever after.

In fiction the Patronesses control who gets a happy ending. The reality was not that far off. An advantageous marriage was one of the most important ways a young woman set herself up for a good future.

But as the Patronesses' lives show, an advantageous marriage was not always a happy marriage. While romance novels require a couple to end up together and happy, the Patronesses of the Regency found their happy endings elsewhere—in the power they maintained through their roles at Almack's.

At the intersection of society and politics, the Patronesses were able to effect change beyond the ballroom. They challenge our notions of what society women were capable of, or even interested in. In their letters, diaries, and biographies, we can see these women use every tool available to achieve their ambitious goals for themselves and their families.

The Patronesses often lived the most scandalous lives of anyone, but their unique position allowed them to protect not only themselves but also the ones they loved. The selection process for the Almack's list occurred every Monday as the seven Patronesses gathered and sat at a long table with three baskets. The baskets were for three different categories of applications: friends, relatives, and near connections; a second basket for accepted applications; and a third for rejections. The third basket had two categories: those who would never be admitted and those who could apply again in the future.

In these baskets we can see the importance of the Patronesses—one had to know them or someone close to them to even be considered for admittance. And while a rejection from admittance could seriously damage someone's social standing, we can also see the room for forgiveness in that third basket.

Almack's and the Patronesses are an integral part of the afterlife of the Regency. They both feature prominently in any number of Regency romance novels, distorted from reality in successive years of fiction. In these depictions we see a germ of truth, but rarely do we get to go deeper and examine the true power the Patronesses wielded.

Recommended Reading/Viewing

Adkins, Roy, and Lesley Adkins. *Jane Austen's England*. Penguin Books, 2014.

Beresford, Chancellor E. *Memorials of St. James's Street, Together with the Annals of Almack's*. G. Richards Ltd., 1922.

Davey, J. "'Wearing the Breeches'? Almack's, the Female Patroness, and Public Femininity c. 1764–1848." *Women's History Review* 26, no. 6 (2016): 822–39. doi: 10.1080/09612025.2016.1203116.

The Duchess (film). Directed by Saul Dibb, 2008.

Erickson, Carolly. *Our Tempestuous Day: A History of Regency England*. William Morrow, 2011.

Gronow, Rees Howell. *Reminiscences of Captain Gronow*. Smith and Elder, 1862.

Heyer, Georgette. *Friday's Child, Cotillion, Regency Buck*. Sourcebooks, 1994.

Kloester, Jennifer. *Georgette Heyer's Regency World*. Sourcebooks, 2010.

Lieven, Dorothea, and Lionel G. Robinson. *Letters of Dorothea, Princess Lieven, During Her Residence in London, 1812–1834*. Longmans, Green, and Co., 1902.

Rendell, Jane. *The Pursuit of Pleasure: Gender, Space, and Architecture in Regency England*. Rutgers University Press, 2002.

Who's Sleeping With Whom

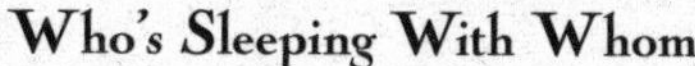

Amelia Stewart, Viscountess of Castlereagh
Frances Villiers, Countess of Jersey
Robert Stewart, Viscount Castlereagh
George IV, King of England
George Villiers, Earl of Jersey
Sarah Villiers, Lady Jersey
Katharina Alexandra Dorothea Fürstin von Lieven
Maria Ponsonby, Viscountess Duncannon
Lady Sarah Villiers
Henry Temple, Viscount Palmerston
Nicholas Paul, Prince Esterhazy
John Ponsonby, Earl of Bessborough
Emily Temple, Viscountess Palmerston
Princess Maria Theresia Esterhazy
William Lamb, Viscount Melbourne
Caroline Lamb
Elizabeth Lamb, Viscountess Melbourne
George Gordon Byron, Baron Byron
KEY
Bold line – related
Line with two arrows – married
Dotted line – affair

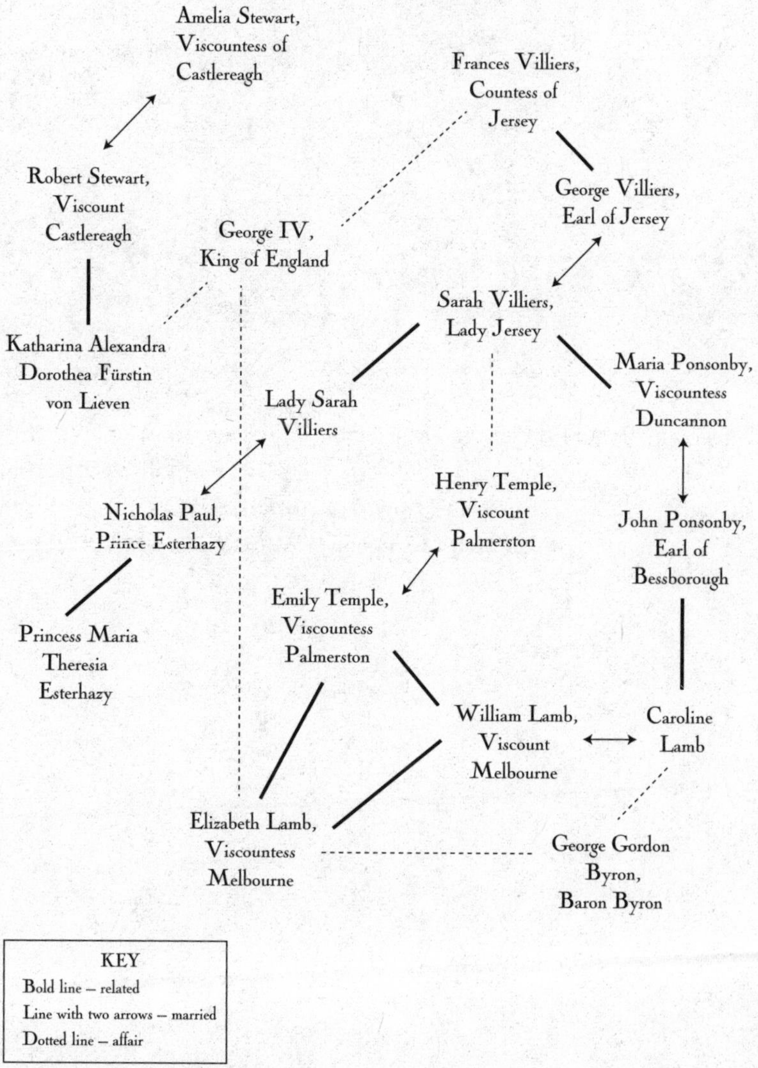

[Figure 1] George Cruikshank. *La belle assemblée or sketches of characteristic dancing.*
Published August 31, 1817, by S. W. Fores, 50 Piccadilly.
(Courtesy of The Lewis Walpole Library, Yale University)

CHAPTER TWO

Game of Thrones

The very name of the Regency era comes from the exchange of power between two royal men—George III and George IV—centering and cementing their roles as the major players in the drama. The royal women are often shunted to the side in this narrative, stripped of their agency.

But the royal women of the Regency are no shrinking violets.

Faced with challenges ranging from not speaking English, to unfaithful and hateful husbands, to parental machinations, these royal women found ways to subvert expectations and live, as much as possible, the lives they wanted.

Of all the many groups of women in this book, the royal women have more of an immediate and obvious connection than any. And yet the network of support among Charlotte of Mecklenburg-Strelitz, Caroline of Brunswick, and Princess Charlotte was fractured at best and nonexistent at worst.

Rather than turn to each other for support, the royal women of the Regency relied on small circles of advisers and confidants, existing in separate spheres. These separate spheres suited the purposes of the royal men of the Regency. George III encouraged his wife, Charlotte of Mecklenburg-Strelitz, to stay out of politics, and George IV had a famously estranged relationship from his wife, Caroline of Brunswick, ignoring her possible political advice entirely. Princess Charlotte was born into this complicated family dynamic, made no easier by her parents' estrangement immediately after her birth. She was used, and often, by both parents in their sparring matches, both public and private.

It is not surprising, then, that the story of the British royal family during the Regency is not a particularly happy one. This is partly due to the true tragedy of King George III's prolonged illness, now believed to be the blood disease porphyria, then seen as madness. Porphyria is a group of disorders resulting from a natural buildup of chemicals that produce porphyrin in the body. Symptoms include hallucinations, paranoia, anxiety, and delusions, all of which George III exhibited during different episodes of his life.

But it's also due to the strained personal relationships among members of the royal family, most famously of course George IV and Caroline of Brunswick's failure of a marriage. The trickle-down effect that broken marriage had can be seen in the lives of all the royal women of the Regency.

George III succeeded to the throne at the age of twenty-two after his grandfather George II passed away unexpectedly. A year later, in 1761, George married Princess Charlotte of Mecklenburg-Strelitz, whom he met on their wedding day. They were crowned together on September 22. The pair enjoyed a fruitful marriage (despite the fact that Charlotte did not speak English upon her arrival to England) and had fifteen children, thirteen of whom survived to adulthood.

Unfortunately, later in life, George III's episodes of instability brought on by his porphyria intensified. The pair's eldest son, the Prince of Wales, was almost named Regent in 1788, but George III recovered before he could take over.

In 1811 the king's health worsened again and the Prince of Wales was officially declared the Prince Regent. He continued in the role until his father's death in 1820, when he officially ascended to the throne and became King George IV.

Unlike his parents, George IV had an abysmally unhappy marriage to Caroline of Brunswick, a wide range of fascinating mistresses, and only one legitimate daughter, Princess Charlotte, who tragically died in childbirth in 1817.

Queen Charlotte of Mecklenburg-Strelitz, Queen Caroline of Brunswick, and Princess Charlotte of Wales too often suffer the fate of other royal women, thrust to the side in favor of discussing their husbands or the men around them. Or they are reduced to their worst moments, especially in Caroline's case, as she lived well outside the bounds of what was socially acceptable or expected for the time, and her reputation paid the price. Charlotte is best remembered for her tragic and early death, but what about the life before that event, which changed history and led directly to Queen Victoria's reign? And while we're often told Queen Charlotte had no interest in politics, over three hundred of her letters survive telling us otherwise.

The royal women of the Regency have suffered the same fate as so many women of the period, reduced to stereotypes and flattened of humanity, but their vibrant, varied lives remind us of their true impact on the period and the importance of this fragmented but indelibly connected network.

CHARLOTTE OF MECKLENBURG-STRELITZ

Sophia Charlotte was born on May 19, 1744, the youngest daughter of Duke Charles Louis Frederick of Mecklenburg and his wife, Princess Elisabeth Albertine of Saxe-Hildburghausen. Charlotte was one of ten children who were all raised in Mirow, now southern Germany. Due to the relative unimportance of the duchy in which she was raised, Charlotte received little of the expected formal education of a future queen of England. She was enrolled in a Protestant convent as a young girl, where she learned French and studied music.

At sixteen, Charlotte was included in the short list of contenders for potential wives for the new king of England, George III, only twenty-two and newly ascended to the throne, but she wasn't considered a top contender until he read a letter she wrote.

In 1760 Charlotte wrote a (widely circulated) letter to Frederick II of Prussia, who had stationed troops in Mecklenburg-Strelitz, Charlotte's home, thus involving the duchy in his wars. Charlotte's letter bemoans the realities of war and hopes for peace:

> I know Sire, that it seems unbecoming in my sex, in this age of vicious refinement, to feel for one's country, to lament the horrors of war, or to wish for the return of peace. I know you may think it more properly my province to study the arts of pleasing, or to turn my thoughts to subjects of a more domestic nature; but however unbecoming it may be in me, I cannot resist the desire of interceding for this unhappy people.[1]

Upon reading the letter, George supposedly turned to a courtier, Lord Harcourt, and said, "This is the lady whom I shall secure for my consort. Here are lasting beauties. The man who has any mind may feast and not be satiated. If the disposition of the Princess but equals her refined sense, I shall be the happiest man, as I hope, with my people's concurrence to be the happiest monarch, in Europe."[2]

In 1761 the king announced to his council his intentions to marry Charlotte, and she traveled from her home to England in a harrowing boat trip. The party encountered several storms that blew them off course, causing the journey to take almost two and a half weeks.

Charlotte was received by the king and his family on her arrival in London on September 6. Upon their meeting, Charlotte sank to her knees, honoring her husband-to-be until he raised her up. They met at 3:30 p.m. and were married later that evening at 9 p.m.

Charlotte's first months in England were difficult as she adjusted to many new things, including an overbearing mother-in-law, Princess Augusta. Despite initially being impressed with Charlotte's letter to the king of Prussia, upon their marriage her husband also ensured that she would have no political role going forward.

Despite these difficulties, Charlotte was determined to have a happy family life. Within a year of being married, she gave birth to her first son, George, Prince of Wales, who would go on to succeed his father as George IV. George was followed by Frederick (1763), William (1765), Charlotte (1766), Edward (1767), Augusta (1768), Elizabeth (1770), Ernest Augustus (1771), Augustus Frederick (1773), Adolphus (1774), Mary (1776), Sophia (1777), Octavius (1779), Alfred (1780), and Amelia (1783).

George took responsibility for the education of the couple's sons, while the daughters' schooling was left up to Charlotte. She took this charge seriously, employing for the girls a range of tutors and governesses who emphasized kindliness and responsibility but also taught them the skills they would be expected to have later in life if they married. George and Charlotte were extremely fond of their daughters and made no moves to arrange advantageous marriages for them, preferring to keep them at home. Unfortunately, this resulted in a great deal of unhappiness for their daughters, who desperately wanted lives and families of their own.

It is historical legend that George told Charlotte not to meddle in English politics and that she generally followed this edict. However, over four hundred letters from Charlotte to her younger brother and confidant Grand Duke Charles II of Mecklenburg-Strelitz survive, along with almost three hundred to her eldest son, George IV. They reveal an intelligent and highly aware ruler who kept careful track of such global events as the American Revolution, discussing England's victories and defeats in her many letters. She also maintained a correspondence and friendship with Queen Marie Antoinette, even preparing apartments for the French royal family if they carried out a plan to flee the French Revolution and take refuge in England.

Charlotte was a keen botanist. She arranged for clippings brought to her by explorers like Captain James Cook to be planted in Kew Gardens, ensuring that those gardens grew and expanded. Charlotte also befriended the writer and artist Mary Delany, arranging for her to receive a pension and inviting her to court to educate the royal children in botany.

Queen Charlotte is of great interest for another reason: her oft-discussed African ancestry. Charlotte was a descendant of Margarita de Castro e Souza, a fifteenth-century Portuguese noblewoman who was herself a descendant of Alfonso III and his mistress Madragana from the thirteenth century. A sixteenth-century Portuguese royal chronicler named Duarte Nunes de Leão wrote that Madragana was a Moor, or person of African descent.

Even more interestingly, Queen Charlotte was painted in 1762 by the Scottish painter Allan Ramsay. [Figure 2] It has been pointed out that, more so than in any other image of her, Charlotte's African heritage has been emphasized, especially in her facial features. It has been suggested that this portrait, and copies of it, were used by abolitionists to further their cause.

Ramsay was not unfamiliar with Africans living in England. His brother-in-law John Lindsay fathered several children with African women and brought one of those children, Dido Elizabeth Belle, to England to be brought up by his uncle, Lord Mansfield. Some have advocated that Ramsay himself could be the painter of a famous portrait of Dido Elizabeth Belle and her cousin Elizabeth Murray.

Regardless, Charlotte's African ancestry seems to have been downplayed in other portraits. She certainly never mentioned it in her many letters to family or other political players.

Whatever her ancestry, Charlotte did not have an easy time as queen of England or wife to the king. Her husband's mental illness made him erratic and sometimes violent, other times smothering. Charlotte had to negotiate with a hostile mother-in-law, who kept details about her husband's health from her, as well as her own son, who stood to gain everything if appointed Regent and nothing if his mother was instead.

In 1811 George III's condition had worsened, and Charlotte was appointed his official guardian under the Regency Bill of 1789, while her son was appointed Prince Regent. Charlotte did not initially agree with the decision to name her son Regent.

Despite their discord, Charlotte still acted as official queen for many royal duties during the Regency due to the Prince Regent's estrangement from his own wife, Caroline of Brunswick.

She was not, however, an innocent bystander in the standoff between her son and daughter-in-law, but an active participant. In May 1814 she wrote to Caroline on her son's instruction, banning her from attending court. "The Queen is thus placed under the painful necessity of intimating to the Princess of Wales, the impossibility of her Majesty's receiving her Royal Highness at her drawing-rooms."[3] Caroline made sure to distribute this letter widely, ensuring that the public was aware of the treatment she was receiving at the hands of her husband and mother-in-law, adding to her popularity and seriously damaging that of George and Charlotte.

Perhaps due to this, Charlotte had a difficult relationship with her granddaughter and namesake, Princess Charlotte. Charlotte (the elder) chose to travel to Bath rather than attend the confinement and birth of her first great-grandchild. However, on the night the baby was stillborn, and Princess Charlotte passed away, Charlotte declared, "I know some fatal event has happened," and was then informed of the tragic news.[4] Charlotte was devastated by the deaths, and her health began to decline rapidly.

Charlotte died while holding her oldest son's hand at Kew Palace in 1818. She didn't live to see the end of the Regency and the start of her son's reign upon her husband's death in 1820.

CAROLINE OF BRUNSWICK

In 1795 Caroline Amelia Elizabeth, Princess of Brunswick, arrived in England to marry the Prince of Wales, who would one day become George IV.

Caroline was born on May 17, 1768, to Charles William Ferdinand, Duke of Brunswick-Wolfenbüttel, and his wife, Princess Augusta of Great Britain. (That's right, Caroline and George were first cousins.) Her lively nature was widely remarked upon. When Lord Malmesbury arrived in Brunswick to bring Caroline back to England and her new life, he was concerned about her lack of polish, writing, "My eternal theme to her... is to think before she speaks, to recollect herself."[5]

Caroline's new husband, George IV, is remembered as a truly terrible ruler, an even worse husband, and a great patron of all the arts. His Regency was marked by his prodigious spending, requiring Parliament to bail him out of debt several times, his marriage to Caroline being one such instance.

George was wildly unpopular, in marked contrast with, and perhaps in part because of his terrible treatment of, his wife.

When Caroline arrived in England to marry George there was a serious impediment: George was already married.

In 1785 he had gone through a marriage ceremony with his mistress Maria Fitzherbert, despite the fact that she was divorced and a Catholic and therefore barred from royal marriage by the Royal Marriages Act of 1772.

Thoughtfully (?) George formally ended his relationship with Maria Fitzherbert by letter before marrying Caroline.

Not so thoughtfully, he rewrote his will the day after Caroline gave birth to their only child, Charlotte, leaving everything to Maria Fitzherbert and a single pound to Caroline.

He also appointed another mistress—Frances Villiers, Countess of Jersey—as his wife's Lady of the Bedchamber. And sent said mistress to welcome his new wife to England! And ride in the carriage with her from Greenwich to London! This situation was not unknown to the public, and was parodied in satirical prints from artists like James Gillray. [Figure 3]

Sources tell us that George was disgusted by his new wife, and that led to his cruel treatment of her. Malmesbury was the only witness to their first meeting, and reported that Caroline tried to kneel before her new husband, who raised her up but then walked off without a word to his bride. He asked Malmesbury to get him a drink and then left to discuss the matter with his mother.

George's unhappiness with his new bride has been much remarked upon, but George didn't do much to impress Caroline, either. She told Malmesbury that the prince was "very fat and he's nothing like as handsome as his portrait."[6]

That evening Caroline was forced to sit at dinner with her husband-to-be and his mistress, Lady Jersey. Three days later Caroline and George married in St. James's Chapel, with George instructing his brother to "tell Mrs. Fitzherbert she is the only woman I shall ever love."[7]

With such an illustrious start to the marriage, is it any wonder that it went from bad to worse? The couple had sex exactly three times (according to George's letters to Malmesbury) and luckily, Caroline got pregnant.

Precisely nine months after their wedding, Caroline gave birth to a baby girl named Charlotte.

The arrival of a much-hoped-for heir did little to thaw relations between Caroline and George. On April 30, 1796, George wrote to Caroline, "Nature has not made us suitable to each other," and indicated his desire for a formal separation.

Caroline agreed with one stipulation: that she would never be forced to have sexual relations with George, even if something happened to Charlotte. He agreed, and the pair separated in 1797.

Caroline settled at Montagu House in Blackheath. For the first time since arriving in England, Caroline was finally free to live life on her own terms. While Blackheath was provincial compared with London, she nevertheless encouraged politicians and important society figures to visit her at her new establishment.

Caroline was a devoted mother to her daughter, Charlotte, with the little girl living near her mother under the care of a governess. But one daughter was not enough for Caroline, who loved children. She began to take in a series of foster children, with the princess overseeing their education. While her heart seems to have been in the right place, the practice of wealthy women taking children from the less-well-off to "ease their burden" is extremely problematic through today's eyes. And there's little evidence about what happened to these children after they left Caroline's household.

Not all of her neighbors approved of Caroline's new lifestyle, in particular Major-General Sir John Douglas and his wife, Lady Charlotte Douglas. Initially friends, the group had a falling-out over Caroline's affection for the Douglases' boarder, Sir Sidney Smith. Caroline and Lady Douglas traded barbs back and forth, and finally Lady Douglas accused Caroline of giving birth to an illegitimate boy (in reality it was one of the foster children Caroline had taken into her home).

King George III was fond of his niece and daughter-in-law, but in 1806 he was forced to look into these allegations with the so-called Delicate Investigation. He was heartily encouraged in this by his son, who had been advised that the only way he would be able to formally and officially divorce his wife was by proving her infidelity.

Led by Prime Minister Lord Grenville, Lord Chancellor Lord Erskine, the Lord Chief Justice of England and Wales Lord Ellenborough, and Home Secretary Lord Spencer, the investigation heard testimony from Lady Douglas and Caroline's servants about her conduct. Lady Douglas testified that Caroline had told her she was pregnant and that the boy was indeed her natural-born son. However, Sophia Austin, the boy's mother, testified that he was her son, contradicting Lady Douglas's testimony. Caroline's servants backed her up, refusing to testify that she had improper relationships with men.

The mere fact that her husband, through careful campaigning publicly and privately, could induce his father to convene such a body of the preeminent men in the country on the strength of mere rumors tells us the lack of balance of power between George and Caroline, and how little control Caroline had over her life or her daughter's. The investigation found that there was no foundation for the allegations, despite George's hopes to the contrary. Regardless, he used the scandal as justification for further separation between Caroline and Charlotte, now requiring a chaperone for their visits.

Caroline had never been particularly popular with the English aristocracy, but the scandal surrounding the Delicate Investigation, along with George's increasingly elaborate parties as he became official Regent, to which she was not invited, contributed to her further isolation.

In January 1813, on the advice of her new champion and friend Henry Brougham, a leading Whig politician, Caroline wrote a letter to George, which was leaked to the press when he refused to respond. In it, Caroline argues against her treatment. The letter was so widely distributed that Jane Austen read it and wrote to her friend Martha Lloyd, "I suppose all the world is sitting in judgement upon the Princess of Wales's letter. Poor woman, I shall support her as long as I can, because she is a Woman and because I hate her Husband..."[8]

In retaliation for the letter, George leaked the details of the Delicate Investigation to the press. Once again, this inflamed public support in favor of Caroline rather than George. But George held the upper hand in one key area, and used the scandal to demand Charlotte be kept from her mother.

In July 1814 George informed Charlotte that she would no

longer be allowed to visit her mother in punishment for breaking her engagement with the Prince of Orange. In response Charlotte ran away to Caroline's house. She was eventually persuaded to return, but Caroline had had enough.

She negotiated with Lord Castlereagh for an annual allowance in return for her leaving the country. Despite her daughter's unhappiness with her decision, Caroline left England for Italy in 1814. She settled in the Villa d'Este on Lake Como, where she established her household. Somewhere along the way she picked up a servant named Bartolomeo Pergami, who quickly became the head of her household and her rumored lover.

The pair traveled throughout the Mediterranean together, causing gossip wherever they were seen. The news reached England via the mouths of many busybodies, including spies that George sent. Lord Sligo wrote at first, "I don't know who is rogering the Princess now," before amending his report to include the news that Pergami "very likely . . . does the job for her."[9]

In 1817 Caroline's beloved daughter Charlotte died in childbirth, and with her, any hope Caroline had of regaining power upon her daughter's accession to the English throne. Caroline's secretary Joseph Hownam had the unfortunate task of telling her. Upon sharing the news Caroline cried and said, "This is not only my last hope gone, but what has England lost?"[10]

With Charlotte's death, George saw a morbid opportunity to once again rid himself of his hated wife. But he still needed grounds, and due to the failure of the Delicate Investigation, he would need a new commission and set of allegations. This time he appointed Vice

Chancellor John Leach to investigate Caroline's adultery. Leach's investigation so terrified Caroline that she agreed to a divorce in exchange for a cash settlement in 1819. Negotiations dragged on, until January 29, 1820, when George III died and George IV officially became king, and Caroline, at least nominally, queen.

Caroline made plans to travel to England to assert her rights as George continued to press for a divorce. The king's ministers advised against it, especially given Caroline's popularity compared with George's increasingly bad reputation.

As George's estranged wife, Caroline became a figurehead for the radical reform movement. When she arrived back in England on June 5, 1820, an enormous crowd greeted her with cheers. Always more popular than George, Caroline served as a convenient rallying cry for those pushing for change in England in the wake of the French Revolution. Caroline corresponded with several leaders in this movement, making them her advisers, including Alderman Matthew Wood and radical MP Sir Francis Burdett. Wood even traveled to Calais to accompany Caroline back to England. This meant that Caroline arrived back in England firmly aligned with his radical politics—at least visually.

George persisted with his bid for a divorce, presenting Parliament with the results of Leach's investigation. This so scandalized the House of Lords that they introduced the Pains and Penalties Bill of 1820, which would dissolve the royal marriage and strip Caroline of her titles. [Figure 4] The bill passed the House of Lords but was never presented in the House of Commons as there was little chance it would pass, due to Caroline's popularity.

While Caroline waited for the trial to get under way, she was shunned by most of England's high society. But there were a few exceptions. Along with Lady Anne Hamilton, a loyal lady-in-waiting, Caroline received one other distinguished visitor: Anne Damer.

Caroline had befriended Anne's own dearest friend Mary Berry upon her arrival in England as a new queen. Because Anne's papers were destroyed on her own order we have no explanation for this remarkable break with high society, but there is an obvious answer. Due to her friendships with women, Anne had faced scandal and social censure for most of her adult life. Perhaps she simply better understood the immense pressure that Caroline was under and wanted to offer her support.

Caroline had one other surprising supporter among the women of the Ton: Sarah Villiers, Lady Jersey. Breaking with her friend then Prince of Wales George IV, her mother-in-law, and many other of the Lady Patronesses of Almack's, Lady Jersey stood by the queen, professing her support publicly.

Despite her precarious position, Caroline pressed ahead with plans to attend George's coronation, despite being told she should not go and would not be admitted if she did show up. On July 19, 1821, at his coronation ceremony George had Caroline turned away from the doors of Westminster. She tried several other entrances and was denied entry at each.

Unfortunately, in that moment public opinion finally turned against her. It's said the crowds jeered her as she was turned away from the coronation service. Caroline never recovered from the humiliation. She fell ill that evening and died a few weeks later on

August 7, 1821. However, she was aware of the seriousness of her illness for several weeks before her death and was able to put her affairs in order. She had many personal papers burned and chose a pointed inscription for her tombstone: CAROLINE OF BRUNSWICK, THE INJURED QUEEN OF ENGLAND.[11]

The Times reported her death on August 8, writing, "The tragedy of the persecutions and death of a QUEEN is at length brought to its awful close; and thousands—we may say millions—of eyes will be suffused with tears when they shall read in this column that CAROLINE OF BRUNSWICK is no more . . . She died as she had lived, a Christian heroine and a martyr."[12]

PRINCESS CHARLOTTE OF WALES

Born on January 7, 1796, into her parents' (then Prince of Wales) George IV and Caroline of Brunswick's deeply unhappy marriage, Princess Charlotte Augusta of Wales was the only child of George IV and the great hope of the Regency period. The poet Leigh Hunt captured the huge expectations of the infant, writing on her birth, "Such a fine young royal creature—Daughter of England!"[13]

From the moment she was born, Charlotte was in a very difficult position. Just a year after her birth, her mother moved out of Carlton House and into her own establishment at Blackheath. Charlotte was shuttled back and forth between them until she turned eight and moved into her own establishment at Warwick House.

This move coincided with an entirely new staff for the young princess. Her father demanded her beloved nanny Lady Elgin resign because she brought Charlotte to visit her grandfather King George III without asking her father for permission.

Her new governess Lady de Clifford brought along her grandson the Honorable George Keppel, who became the princess's childhood friend and later wrote a memoir about their time together.

Along with Lady de Clifford, Charlotte's education was entrusted to the Bishop of Exeter. The pair fought constantly over what the princess should be taught, and how. Rounding out this group was the Reverend Dr. George Nott, the princess's chaplain, along with two subgovernesses. Charlotte also received special education from experts in a number of subjects, particularly excelling at the piano under the tutelage of Jane Mary Guest, herself a student of Johann Christian Bach.

Eventually Nott was replaced by the Reverend Dr. William Short. Short introduced Charlotte to his niece, the Honorable Margaret Mercer Elphinstone. "Dearest Miss Mercer" became Charlotte's best friend and confidante for the rest of her life.

This staff was Charlotte's adopted family. She said as much in a childhood will she wrote in 1806; all of ten years old, she leaves almost all her earthly possessions to her staff members, with a brief mention of "my father and mother, the Prince and Princess of Wales," who are left her most valuable jewels.

That same year, relations between Charlotte's parents broke down even further as George insisted that the government investigate his wife's supposed infidelity in what came to be known as the Delicate Investigation. Charlotte was forbidden from seeing her mother during the investigation, and her own grandfather, the king, refused to receive her.

Used as a pawn by the adults in her life from the earliest possible age, is it any wonder that contemporaries described Charlotte as undignified and wild? After visiting Windsor in 1809 Lady Albinia Cumberland wrote, "I do not think her manner dignified, as a Princess's ought to be, or, indeed, as I should wish a daughter of mine to behave."[14] Of course, other visitors were kinder. The Grand Duchess Catherine was quite taken with Charlotte when she visited England, writing that she was "the most interesting member of the [royal] family..."[15] But Catherine also shared Lady Campbell's concerns about Charlotte's manners: "She is ravishing, and it is a crime to have allowed her to acquire such habits."[16]

As her father was busy with his duties as Prince Regent, Charlotte spent more and more time at Windsor with her aunts. There she formed an attachment to her illegitimate cousin George FitzClarence, son of her uncle the Duke of Clarence. After George was called to join his regiment in Brighton, Charlotte's attentions moved to another rumored illegitimate cousin, Charles Hesse, an officer in the Light Dragoons.

Charlotte was encouraged in her love affairs by her mother, Caroline, who allowed the couple to meet in her apartments. Caroline and Charlotte also used Hesse as a courier for their letters, a perfect arrangement for all concerned. But once again, war interfered and Hesse left to serve in Spain, ending the love affair.

As always, Charlotte was caught between her parents and their machinations. And this extended beyond her love life. As a young man, George was a professed Whig. Caroline allowed her loyalties to shift more fluidly, taking advice from whoever was in opposition to her husband at any given moment. However, it was a Tory government that named George Prince Regent, handing him the power he had desperately wanted his whole life.

After his appointment, it was expected that he would dismiss the government and call for a general election, ushering in an era of Whig rule. But the prince decided against calling an election, betraying the Whigs, and his daughter.

Charlotte was a devoted Whig. In this she was supported and encouraged by her friend Mercer Elphinstone, much to her father's displeasure. And Charlotte decided to make it known with a public display of support to Earl Grey, leader of the Whig party and the opposition. Charlotte spotted him at the opera and leaned out of her box to blow kisses at him, for all the world to see and report on.

It wasn't the first or last time the Whigs and Tories used Charlotte's awful position between her parents as fodder for their political goals. George was insistent on treating Charlotte as a child, forbidding her from attending many social functions and famously telling her, "Depend upon it, as long as I live you shall never have an establishment, unless you marry."[17] Caroline was busy with her own unfortunate position, and had little time to truly help her daughter better her life.

Luckily, some hope appeared in 1813, as the Prince Regent finally turned his attention to the question of Charlotte's future husband. Charlotte had clearly come to understand that the only way she would gain some semblance of independence and control over her life was through marriage.

For a number of reasons, all political and none having to do with love or Charlotte's future happiness, George landed on William, Hereditary Prince of Orange, as a suitable potential husband.

Unfortunately the first meeting did not go well, as William got drunk with the Prince Regent. Caroline did not approve of the match, and public sentiment was against it as well. Charlotte was primarily concerned about being forced to leave England as its monarch wed to the monarch of another country.

Nonetheless, negotiations continued, and in 1814 Charlotte signed a marriage contract.

That didn't mean she was done fighting for control of her future and the choice of who she would marry.

Charlotte told the Prince of Orange that once they were married, she would of course receive her mother in their home.

The Prince of Orange was in a no-win situation. His soon-to-be father-in-law, the one-day king of England, would never accept his new son-in-law receiving his estranged wife, and the prince told Charlotte as much.

Who promptly broke off the engagement.

Charlotte had shown not only her father, but the entire country, that she would make her own decisions, consequences be damned.

In punishment George barred Charlotte from visiting her mother, causing Charlotte to run away to her mother's house. There she gathered her advisers, who rather than giving her the advice she wanted, sent her back to her father.

After an emotional reunion, George sent Charlotte to Cranbourne Lodge where she was under strict observation. She quickly complained to her uncle, the Duke of Sussex, who then made public inquiries about Charlotte's well-being to the prime minister, Lord Liverpool, in the House of Lords. The Prince Regent was so furious he never spoke to his brother again.

After Charlotte's mother, Caroline, left England for Italy in 1814, the Prince Regent finally allowed Charlotte to leave Cranbourne for the seaside town of Weymouth. While there, crowds showed up in displays of support.

She may have been free, but the question of her marriage still wasn't settled. Unhappy with her other prospects, Charlotte fixated on Prince Leopold of Saxe-Coburg-Saalfeld, whom she had met a year earlier. While her father did not initially take the impoverished prince's proposal seriously, when faced with mass opposition to his choice, the Prince of Orange, George finally relented and invited Prince Leopold to Brighton for an interview in February 1816. George was impressed with the prince and Charlotte wrote that he had told her that Leopold "had every qualification to make a woman happy."[18]

On March 14, 1816, an announcement was made in the House of Commons. Parliament voted Leopold £50,000 a year, and bought the couple Claremont House and Camelford House.

Charlotte and Leopold were married May 2, 1816, in Carlton House. The newlyweds were wildly popular and appeared frequently in London society after their honeymoon.

Princess Lieven, Patroness of Almack's and noted leader of

society, wrote in a letter to her brother Alexander, "Princess Charlotte is happy and contented; they are both of them prodigiously in love—he with his wife, and she with her husband and freedom."[19]

Charlotte wrote to her best friend Mercer that Leopold was "the perfection of a lover."[20]

A few months after the wedding, Charlotte fell ill. She was unable to attend the opera or the final performance of the celebrated actress Sarah Siddons. Her doctor finally announced that Charlotte had miscarried.

She seemed to recover quickly, and with her the press and public recovered their belief that the princess would one day give birth to a healthy child. Privately Charlotte was devastated, and wrote to her mother, despite her father's edict that the pair not communicate, "Why is not my mother allowed to pour cheerfulness into the sinking heart of her inexperienced and trembling child?...I have but one mother."[21]

Happily, in April 1817 Prince Leopold informed the Prince Regent that Charlotte was pregnant again and the doctors believed there was no reason she wouldn't have a healthy birth. This good news was sorely needed in England, which was suffering an economic recession after the Napoleonic Wars.

Charlotte's pregnancy was followed obsessively by the press. It was calculated that the birth of a princess would raise the stock market 2.5 percent, while the birth of a prince would raise it 6 percent.[22]

In August 1817 Charlotte was put under medical care, with Sir Richard Croft, an accoucheur rather than a physician, leading her medical team. Even the choice of her doctor was a subject of intense speculation and discussion. Along with Croft, consultant Dr. John Sims and nurse Mrs. Griffiths were appointed to Charlotte's care team.

Dr. Croft put Charlotte on a diet immediately and began to bleed her regularly. Leopold's private physician and friend Dr. Stockmar was appalled at this treatment, pointing out that it was no longer considered healthy in the rest of Europe.

On Monday, November 4, Charlotte went into labor, promising Mrs. Griffiths, "I will neither bawl nor shriek."[23]

Charlotte labored for fifty hours to give birth to a stillborn son. As Mrs. Griffiths and the other maids wept, Charlotte tried to comfort them.

A few hours later, never truly recovering, Charlotte died. Upon being brought to see his dead wife, Leopold turned to his friend Stockmar and whispered, "I am now quite desolate. Promise to stay with me always."[24]

With those words, Leopold captured the sentiment of the entire country. As Lady Charlotte Bury wrote, "There is now no object of great interest in the English people, no one great rallying point round which all parties are ready to join... A greater public calamity could not have occurred to us; nor could it have happened at a more unfortunate moment."[25]

The public mourning for the Princess of Wales was widespread. The Prince Regent was so grief-stricken he couldn't attend the funeral. Dr. Croft committed suicide because he blamed himself for being unable to save the princess.

Charlotte's death set off a mad scramble among the surviving royal dukes to leave their mistresses and provide the elderly King George III with a legitimate heir. In 1818 Prince Edward, Duke of Kent and Strathearn, married Prince Leopold's widowed sister Princess Victoria; a year later the pair welcomed their daughter Victoria, who would inherit the English throne in 1837.

Victoria would rule for sixty-three years, making her the longest-reigning monarch up to that point. Her uncle Leopold was a trusted adviser and even introduced Victoria to his nephew Prince Albert of Saxe-Coburg and Gotha, her future husband. Victoria ruled over a period of huge expansion for the British Empire, and her reign was markedly different from her profligate uncle's. Victoria, along with the support and help of Albert, tried to make the royal family and by extension court a moral center for the country.

Leopold never forgot Charlotte, considering her the great and only love of his life. He named his first daughter with his second wife Charlotte. And for Victoria's twenty-sixth birthday he sent her a portrait of his beloved Charlotte, writing, "Grant always to that good and generous Charlotte—who sleeps already with her beautiful little boy so long—an affectionate remembrance, and believe me, she deserves it."[26]

CONCLUSION

While they might have had wealth and stature, the royal women of the Regency did not have an easy road to walk. And even that wealth and that stature could be very much in question depending on how much in favor—with the royal men and the public—they were at any given moment.

The royal women of the Regency came blaring back into the public consciousness in 2016 when Prince Harry of England announced that he was dating the American biracial actress Meghan Markle.

Almost immediately Meghan was subjected to racist coverage in the British press, and Harry sought to defend her by releasing a public statement confirming their relationship and condemning the "wave of abuse and harassment" that Meghan had endured.[27]

Another round of defense came from historians who pointed out that Meghan would not be the first member of the English royal family with African heritage—Queen Charlotte of Mecklenburg-Strelitz holds that honor.

Time magazine, the *Washington Post*, and others reported widely on this historical precedent. It even made its way into pop-culture pieces about Meghan and Harry's relationship—like the Lifetime original movie *Meghan and Harry: Becoming Royal* (2018). In the film, as Meghan and Harry face increasingly negative press for their relationship, they turn to Harry's grandmother Queen Elizabeth II for support. Queen Elizabeth cheerily brushes off their worries and informs them both, "Oh yes, you're of mixed race, Harry. So am I," as the trio stand in front of the Ramsay portrait of Queen Charlotte. "I've always loved this portrait of Queen Charlotte because the painter Ramsay didn't try to hide her African heritage . . . Many of her portraits try to hide that fact, but this one is most authentic, just like you."

Recommended Reading

Behrendt, Stephen. *Royal Mourning and Regency Culture*. Macmillan, 1997.

Chambers, James. *Charlotte and Leopold: The True Story of the Original People's Princess*. Old Street Publishing, 2007.

Jeffries, Sabrina. Royal Brotherhood Series: *In the Prince's Bed* (2004), *To Pleasure a Prince* (2005), *One Night with a Prince* (2005). Pocket Books.

Kelly, Vanessa. Renegade Royals Series: *Lost in a Royal Kiss* (2013), *Secrets for Seducing a Royal Bodyguard* (2013), *Confessions of a Royal Bridegroom* (2014), *Tall, Dark and Royal* (2014), *How to Plan a Wedding for a Royal Spy* (2015), *How to Marry a Royal Highlander* (2015), *The Buccaneer Duke* (2018). Zebra Publishing.

Norton, Elizabeth. *England's Queen: A Biography*. Amberley Publishing, 2011.

Plowden, Alison. *Caroline and Charlotte: Regency Scandals*. History Press, 2011.

Robins, Jane. *Rebel Queen: The Trial of Queen Caroline*. Simon and Schuster, 2006.

Williams, Kate. *Becoming Queen Victoria: The Tragic Death of Princess Charlotte and the Unexpected Rise of Britain's Greatest Monarch*. Ballantine Books, 2008.

[Figure 2] Allan Ramsay. *Queen Charlotte in coronation robes*. 1761–1769. Royal Collection Trust.
(Royal Collection Trust/© Her Majesty Queen Elizabeth II 2019)

[Figure 3] James Gillray.
"The Jersey Smuggler detected; —or—Good causes for discontent."
Published May 24, 1796, by H. Humphrey, New Bond Street.
(Courtesy of The Lewis Walpole Library, Yale University)

[Figure 4] *A Royal salute.*
Published August 28, 1820, by S. W. Fores, 41 Picadilli.
(Courtesy of The Lewis Walpole Library, Yale University)

CHAPTER THREE

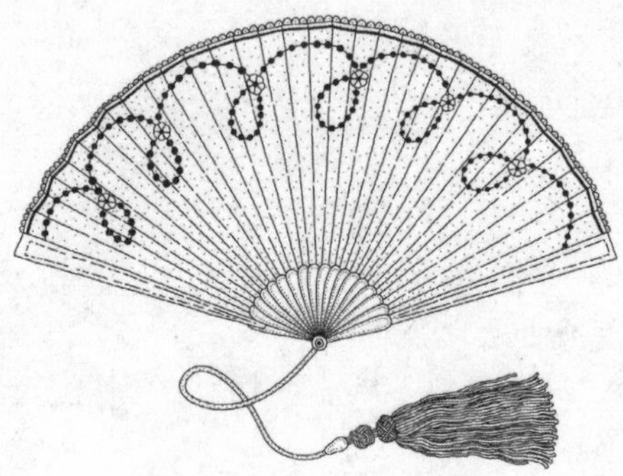

Mistresses

The Regency has a decidedly sexy reputation. Regency-set romance novels are partly responsible, and these works focus almost entirely on a couple who end up married. Sure, they have plenty of sex along the way (or after the fact), but marriage is the expected goal of a heterosexual Regency couple, and one that we are told, in turn, leads to hot sex.

In truth, a lot of the sex happening during the Regency was firmly outside the bonds of marriage. Infidelity, especially among the upper classes, was rampant.

The 1770s brought a change in attitudes toward adultery, widely attributed to the royal family's profligacy. There was a perception, perhaps true, that adultery was now much more widespread throughout the upper classes. This perception was helped along by newspapers and satirical broadsheets that reported on the sexual affairs of the Ton. In 1769 *Town and Country* began publishing the infamous "Tête-à-Tête" series—which ran for twenty-four years—salaciously detailing these affairs. This content was devoured by Regency audiences of all classes.

And George IV, first as the Prince of Wales and then as king, set a new standard for mistresses, sleeping with many of his friends' wives, popular actresses, seemingly anyone but his wife, whom he detested. His almost constant search for a reason to divorce her meant that even the most royal woman in the country wasn't safe from (very public) accusations of infidelity.

Many of the women in these pages had affairs outside their marriages. So who ends up in this chapter devoted solely to "Mistresses" with a capital *M*?

These are women who have become known to and immortalized in history as sexual partners.

Sadly, they're often reduced simply to a famous affair, the rest of their lives discarded as unnecessary or uninteresting to the greater narrative. But three of the four mistresses in this chapter were also published authors, and the fourth was an artist in her own right. These women lived full lives outside the bedroom, but that is where history has left them. Their affairs color every other facet of those lives, even after they're long over.

It is striking and noteworthy that so many of these supposed fallen women refused to stay silent in their shame. Instead they wrote their own stories, sometimes with a thin veil of fiction, in their own words.

Narratively, the mistress is supposed to fade into the background after the happy couple has finally found their way to each other. By centering themselves in memoirs, poetry, novels, and on the stage, these mistresses chose a different path. They demand that we contend with them both inside and outside the bedroom, never sugarcoating the truth but refusing to be typecast as the other woman.

MARY DARBY ROBINSON

Mary Robinson was and is known as Perdita because that's the role she played when George IV, then Prince of Wales, saw her and fell madly in love, setting off his first famous love affair and Mary's lifelong notoriety.

But Mary was more than just a royal mistress to be used and discarded. She was also a talented writer who wrote essays, two plays, seven novels, and hundreds of poems. As a celebrated beauty of the era, Mary had her likeness rendered by many major artists of the period including Gainsborough, Romney, and Reynolds. And she was not simply a subject but also an active participant in the creation of her image. While she might have had a steep learning curve, Mary kept careful tabs on her public image and worked hard to shape a narrative through the images she sat for and the words she wrote.

She was born in 1758 (according to her diaries; other sources put her birth in the year 1756) to naval captain Nicholas Darby and his wife, Hester. Darby was a member of the Society of Merchant Venturers, and spent long stretches of time abroad. In contrast, Hester was a doting mother who spoiled her children. Mary was lucky enough to grow up in Bristol, where the More sisters, Hannah and Mary, had set up a private school to educate young women in "French, Reading, Writing, Arithmetic, and Needlework."[1] Mary attended this school, much to Hannah More's later chagrin, as she became more and more conservative and regretted her connection to such an infamous woman.

In 1765 Darby set sail for America to set up a whale fishery, effectively separating from Hester.

Upon his return to England, Darby summoned his estranged wife and children to London. It was decided that Mary would continue her schooling at Lorrington Academy in Chelsea, under the care of Meribah Lorrington, whom Mary credits with teaching her everything she would use in her later literary career. When Darby ran into financial troubles and stopped paying for Mary's education, Hester opened her own school to teach her daughter and earn money. Mary helped, teaching English and "moral lessons." Darby was so embarrassed that his wife was working that he ordered the school shut down.

Mary was drawn to the stage from an early age. She remembered seeing her first play *King Lear,* and the famous actor David Powell in the titular role. After her parents' separation her mother began a relationship with Samuel Cox, a lawyer. Cox was friendly with Dr. Samuel Johnson and through him, fourteen-year-old Mary gained an introduction to David Garrick.

David Garrick took an immediate interest in Mary. He was well known as a supporter of young women in the theater, helping actresses and playwrights alike. Mary quickly became known as Garrick's new protégée, much to her mother's concern.

After pressure from her mother, Mary married Thomas Robinson, who was studying to be a lawyer and claimed to have an inheritance. No inheritance ever materialized, and Mary found herself married to a man who was still training in his career, with no real income to speak of. Worst of all, due to her marriage, Mary had to give up her planned career on the stage. However, Garrick received the news with aplomb and remained a friend and supporter, despite the ruin of his plans for Mary.

In the early days of their marriage, Thomas refused to publicly acknowledge his new wife. Furthermore, the couple were dealing with money problems that required a loan from a friend, John King, a Jewish moneylender. The letters that Mary and John exchanged would come back to haunt her later in life. (John King's daughters Charlotte and Sophia would grow up to be huge fans of Mary Robinson's poetry and emulate her in their own literary careers.)

The young couple moved to London and set up house, spending lavishly despite their earlier problems. Mary quickly found a circle of friends and admirers. But Thomas continued to gamble, drink, and womanize, even after Mary learned she was pregnant.

On October 18, 1774, Mary gave birth to a daughter, Maria Elizabeth Robinson. Three weeks later the couple had to flee

Trevecca House where Mary had given birth because Thomas's creditors had caught up with him. The authorities arrested Thomas at Mary's grandmother's house in Monmouth.

The young family returned to London, where Thomas was able to take care of the debt. And for a few weeks it looked like they would resume their old lives. Mary began making preparations to publish her first book of poetry. But Thomas was once again arrested, and on May 3, 1775, he was committed to the Fleet jail. It was not required for wives to join their husbands in jail, but Mary chose to join Thomas in the Fleet. She also chose to bring Maria, refusing to be separated from her young baby.

While in prison, Mary worked hard to make money to secure their release. She published her first book, *Poems by Mrs. Robinson*, in 1775. Her longest poem, *Captivity*, was about her time in debtors' prison. This second volume was dedicated to Georgiana, Duchess of Devonshire, with permission, "the friendly Patroness of the Unhappy."[2]

Out of jail and once again looking for a means to support her family, Mary returned to her dreams of a stage career. Desperately needing the money, Thomas saw his initial misgivings vanish. Mary made the acquaintance of playwright and theater manager Richard Sheridan, who told his friend Garrick that the girl he had once hoped to introduce on stage would now actually be making her debut. Garrick came out of retirement to train her.

Mary made her debut as Juliet in 1776. "The thundering applause that greeted me nearly overpowered all my faculties," she remembered later in her memoir.[3]

In 1779 Mary appeared in the role that would define her life: Perdita in *Florizel and Perdita*, an adaptation of Shakespeare's *A Winter's Tale*. The royal family attended the theater at Drury Lane on December 3. The seventeen-year-old Prince of Wales sat separately from his parents in the prince's box. After the final curtsy, Mary wrote, their eyes met and "with a look that I shall never forget, he gently inclined his head a second time; I felt the compliment, and blushed my gratitude."[4]

George wrote to his first love, his sister's governess Mary Hamilton, that he had fallen in love with someone else (and therefore must end their attachment). "Her name is Robinson, on or off the stage for I have seen her both, she is I believe almost the greatest and most perfect beauty of her sex."[5]

Using Lord Malden as a go-between, George began sending Mary love letters written as Florizel and addressed to his Perdita.

Every detail of the love affair was published in the newspapers. [Figure 5] The *Morning Post* wrote on July 18, "In the last solemn season of Lent, whenever Florizel was present at the Oratorio, Perdita never failed to testify her taste for sacred music, or something else, by being there also."[6] Mary's celebrity status was cemented by the affair, despite the fact that it only lasted a year.

The Prince of Wales made many promises to her during that year, but he reneged on every last one of them, especially the monetary ones. Mary decided to make the best of a bad situation, demanding £25,000 for the return of incriminating letters from the prince. Lord Malden (the original assistant to the affair) and Charles James Fox (a powerful politician who slept with everyone) negotiated on Mary's behalf, leading to rumors that she was now sleeping with them both.

If the first part of Mary's life was defined in history by her association with the Prince of Wales, the latter part was marked by another relationship, Mary's with Banastre Tarleton.

Banastre was a poor but highly decorated military officer who appeared in the Prince of Wales's social circle in 1782. This circle lived fast and expensively, and Banastre barely had the capital to engage.

One night Mary's friend and rumored lover Lord Malden bet Banastre that Mary would stay faithful to him, even if Banastre attempted to seduce her.

Lord Malden lost the bet several weeks later.

When Mary found out she was furious, but didn't break off her liaison with Banastre. Instead the pair began a relationship that would last fifteen years.

Banastre's family was horrified at his new lover, and offered him a considerable sum of money, enough to pay off his debts, on the condition that he leave for the Continent and leave Mary behind in England as well. Mary, pregnant with Banastre's child, tried to raise money to pay off the debts herself, but it was to no avail. Banastre left for France in 1783. In her attempts to get him to stay Mary underwent a dangerous journey to Dover to intercept him, and suffered a miscarriage. Her health care in the aftermath was so poor that she suffered lasting effects for the rest of her life.

Banastre finally returned to England in 1784 and the couple picked up where they had left off. Mary helped him edit and revise the military history he had worked on while in France. After a joint move to France to stave off creditors, Banastre published his book *A History of the Campaigns of 1780 and 1781*, which was critically well received but made little money. Once again they returned to England, where Mary published a new collection titled *Poetry*. The subscriber list included the Prince of Wales as well as Mary's early patron Georgiana, Duchess of Devonshire, and reflected Mary's continuing importance and fascination for the members of the Ton.

In 1785 Robert Merry had gathered a group of fellow poets together to publish an anthology of poetry titled *The Florence Miscellany*. The poets called themselves the Della Cruscans. Mary admired their style and began to publish poetic responses to Robert Merry's and others' poems in a new newspaper, the *World*. It was in one such poem that she accused Banastre of infidelity and feared for the end of their relationship.

That year also saw Banastre Tarleton finally call off his years-long relationship with Mary and marry heiress Susan Priscilla Bertie, herself the illegitimate daughter of the Duke of Ancaster.

In 1799 Mary published a work of social criticism titled *A Letter to the Women of England, on the Injustice of Mental Subordination* in which she praised her friend, the recently deceased feminist Mary Wollstonecraft. The piece calls for women to be treated as equal partners in marriage and attacks the law that gave a woman's property to her husband upon marriage. This kind of subversive writing is so rarely a part of Mary Robinson's story, but that would come as no surprise to Mary. She wrote at the end of the *Letter*, "There are men who affect, to think light of the literary production of women; and yet no works of the present day are so universally read as theirs."[7]

Mary published a number of novels during her lifetime, many of which were well received. She also tried her hand at writing plays, but her only performed work, *Nobody*, written to showcase the comedic talents of actress Dora Jordan, was a failure after only three performances.

In the last year of her life, struggling with ill health, she took over as poetry editor for the *Morning Post*.

Like so many of the brilliant, prescient women in this book, Mary turned her attention to writing her own memoirs at the end of her life. Sadly, she died in 1800 before finishing them, but her daughter Maria finished and published them a year later. In declaring the news of her death the *Morning Post* wrote, "The literary world have to regret the loss of Mrs. Robinson, who died on Friday morning at eight o'clock, at her cottage on Englefield Green…In her last moments however, she was consoled by the tender attentions of her daughter and of many friends, who deeply lament that a woman of so much genius, of such an elegant taste, of so rich an imagination in poetry, should be cut off at a period when the mental faculties are in their prime."[8]

GRACE DALRYMPLE ELLIOTT

Grace Dalrymple Elliott was the mistress to not one but two royal men, one English, the other French. She traveled back and forth between England and France, surviving the French Revolution and living to write about all her adventures.

Born in Edinburgh around 1754, Grace was the youngest child

of Grisel Craw and Hew Dalrymple, who separated soon after her birth. Grace was most likely raised by her grandparents and then educated at a French convent. She returned to Edinburgh and was introduced into society by her father. Her beauty made quite an impression, and in 1771 she accepted an offer to marry Dr. John Elliott. Elliott's wealth and position made up for their twenty-year age difference.

While the marriage started out happily enough, it quickly turned sour. Both parties were unfaithful, and news quickly spread. In 1774 *Town and Country* began reporting on rumblings of infidelity, writing that the doctor had been crowned with "hymeneal honours"[9]—a reference to Hymen, the bisexual god of marriage and love who was honored by a hymn sung to couples outside the bridal bedroom.

As is so often the case, Grace received most of the public shame and scorn for her affairs, especially after Elliott sued her lover Lord Valentia for criminal conversation—in other words, adultery.

The case took three years, but Elliott won, receiving £12,000 in damages and obtaining a divorce.

The entire thing was humiliating and extremely public. The Elliotts' servants were called in to testify, one after another, that they had seen Grace with Lord Valentia on many occasions, and that she had often returned home "much tumbled, and her Hair loose."[10]

Grace was sent to the country for several months to ruminate on her sins and then to a convent in Paris. She was cast out of her home, family, and polite society.

Dr. Elliott, on the other hand, was knighted, created a baronet, and made one of the personal physicians to the Prince of Wales.

It is rumored that Grace met her next lover, Lord Cholmondeley, in Paris after she left the convent. And what else was she supposed to do but find a wealthy lover to take care of her? Grace had no money, no family to help her, and no education in a workable trade.

The only avenue available to her, indeed to many divorced women in the early nineteenth century, was to join the demi-monde, or the world of women who traded sex and companionship for protection and money.

While women of the demi-monde existed in the same social spaces as women of high society, it was a very different life from the one Grace had been brought up to live. Rather than the stability of a husband, Grace was at the mercy of her lovers and their whims.

Luckily, Grace's first official protector after the divorce, Lord Cholmondeley, was a popular and powerful peer, and the pair seemed to have had a genuine affection for each other that carried on through the rest of their lives. Unfortunately for Grace, Cholmondeley had no intention of marrying his mistress (unlike several of his peers, most notably the Earl of Derby who married his actress mistress Eliza Farren).

In 1779 Grace left Cholmondeley and England to try her luck on the Continent. Having spent time in a French convent as a child, Grace already spoke French and understood the ways of the French aristocracy. She was an instant hit on her arrival in Paris, and her name was linked with a number of influential and aristocratic men.

Ever ambitious in her choice of lovers, Grace ended up with Louis-Philippe, then the Duc de Chartres, later the Duc d'Orléans. For three years Grace ruled over a large house in Paris as an official mistress. But the duke's attentions were fickle, and after three years Grace returned to England, right into the arms of George IV, then Prince of Wales.

George had recently broken up with another mistress, Elizabeth Armistead, so Grace's timing could not have been more perfect. For a few months in the summer of 1781, Grace was the favorite mistress of the Prince of Wales.

As the prince lost interest with the turning of the leaves, Grace became pregnant. She publicly claimed the child was his in the *Morning Post* and also said that the prince took responsibility for the child. Henry Bate Dudley, the editor of the *Morning Herald*, wrote about the baby and question of paternity, "However difficult it may be to ascertain its real sire, one is already named for it, who is said to be extremely flattered by the novelty of the title, and has already given orders that the ceremonies of the straw be supported with the utmost magnificence and eclat."[11]

Privately, he seems to have believed that Lord Cholmondeley was the father, but the baby was baptized Georgiana Augusta Frederica Elliott (the prince's full name was George Augustus Frederick), and Grace named the prince as the father on the baptism register. The girl was raised as a ward of Lord Cholmondeley, and he made sure she was cared for the rest of her life. He ensured that she was accepted by high society, despite the shadow around her birth, and negotiated her marriage settlement with a highly respectable match: Lord William Francis Charles James Augustus Cavendish-Bentinck, the son of the third Duke of Portland.

It was not unusual for young children to be raised separately from their parents, especially if the mother was not an official wife. Grace's life was insecure. She had to move around with her lovers, or find new ones. Perhaps due to this, or perhaps due to the Prince of Wales's interference, Georgiana was raised by Cholmondeley and his family in relative luxury and safety. Grace visited her as often as she could.

In 1784 Grace left England and returned to France and her former lover, the Duc d'Orléans. She stayed there for the next ten years, living through the French Revolution, and surviving, unlike many of her aristocratic circle.

Having spent many years watching newspapers drag her name through the mud and build a narrative around her life, Grace kept a journal where she wrote down her perspective on events. This journal, titled *Journal of My Life During the French Revolution*, was published after her death in 1859 thanks to the efforts of Grace's granddaughter Georgiana Cavendish-Bentinck.

Unlike her lover, who later took the name Philippe Égalité, Grace was a royalist sympathizer. She worked behind the scenes to ensure the safety of a number of aristocrats, at great personal risk. More recently, historians have begun to acknowledge and research the role Grace played as a spy and courier between France and England during and after the Revolution.

She was certainly personally responsible for the safe escape of several aristocrats, including the Marquis de Champcenetz and

Madame de Périgord and her children. She also acted as courier for Marie Antoinette, bringing a letter she wrote to her sister, the Archduchess Maria Christina in Brussels in 1790. Grace also made several trips back and forth to the Belgian town of Spa.

On April 4, 1793, Grace was arrested after a search of her home turned up letters to Charles James Fox, the famous British politician. "They told me they had long suspected me, but that now they had found out that I was in correspondence with the enemies of the Republic, and that I should pay dearly for it."[12] She was imprisoned for eighteen months in four separate prisons and finally released. It wasn't the last time she would be arrested, questioned, and imprisoned during the Terror. But Grace always found a way out, through either her own charms or her influential friends pulling strings.

Shortly after a preliminary peace treaty was signed at Amiens in 1801, Grace returned to England. She bounced back and forth between France and England, depending on friends for financial assistance as the prince continued to be less than prompt with his annuity payments. Inheritances from an aunt and an old friend allowed Grace to live out the rest of her years in some comfort, and provide a part of the marriage settlement for her beloved daughter.

In 1808 Grace's daughter Georgiana got married. We have no evidence that Grace attended the wedding, but she did meet her granddaughter, Georgiana, born in 1811. Georgiana (the elder) died two years later, and Grace returned to France upon her daughter's death.

The last years of Grace's life were very different from her earlier public years. She disappeared from the public record, and her last residence is unknown. In 1822 Grace wrote her will. She settled her debts to a friend, left money and a gold watch to her godson, and willed the rest to her granddaughter, Georgiana. Grace died a year later on May 15, 1823.

EMMA HAMILTON

One of the true rags-to-riches stories of the Regency, Amy Lyon was born on April 26, 1765. She would go on to change her name and become Emma Hamilton, one of the most famous and celebrated beauties of her time, and notorious for her role as mistress to not one but two famous men.

Emma's father died two months after she was born, and her mother, Mary Cadogan, returned to her own mother's home to raise her infant daughter.

Emma entered service at the age of twelve as a maid, and if her life had continued as expected from there the historical record would have forgotten her. As it was, Emma met another maid named Jane Powell who dreamed of being an actress and encouraged Emma in her own ambitions. To that end, Emma took a position as a maid at the Covent Garden Theatre in London, alongside stars like Mary Robinson.

Emma, beautiful and imbued with a natural grace, soon found work as a model and dancer at the Temple of Health, a quack medical establishment founded by the Scottish doctor James Graham. At the Temple, Graham displayed an electromagnetic apparatus surrounded by his "Goddesses of Health" (in reality, young models and actresses) and provided various therapies to his patients. His treatments were especially popular with women struggling with fertility.

Emma was a favorite of the male patrons, and entered into a series of increasingly complicated love affairs, the details of which often take up all the space given to Emma by history. She had a daughter, Emma Carew, who was fostered out though Emma tried to maintain a relationship with her and ensured she was provided for, at least financially, her entire life.

One of Emma's lovers, the Honorable Charles Greville, arranged for her to sit for George Romney, one of the most important and fashionable artists of the Regency period. Emma, as painted by Romney, became one of the most iconic beauties of the Regency. There is something deeply engrossing and mysterious about the dark-eyed beauty that Romney and Emma presented to the world, especially after he began painting her as various classical figures. It is easy to see why she was the subject of such fascination. [Figure 6]

Despite her beauty and celebrity, Greville soon tired of their association and sent Emma to Naples in 1786, ostensibly on a long holiday. In actuality, Greville had sent Emma to his uncle, Sir William Hamilton, the recently widowed British envoy to Naples, as a potential new mistress. Emma was not informed of the men's plans.

Emma was furious when she realized what Greville had done. But she was charmed by the intense attentions Sir William paid her, and they fell in love. Ignoring the previous plans about mistresses, they were married on September 6, 1791, in London after receiving the king's permission. The groom was sixty and the bride was twenty-six.

The newlyweds returned to Naples and Emma, as the newly titled Lady Hamilton, began a career as an ambassador's wife. She befriended Queen Maria Carolina, sister of Marie Antoinette, and in doing so secured her acceptance by the highest social circles in Naples.

Emma was also a talented singer, who used this time to work on her craft. She was so noted for her abilities that the Royal Opera in Madrid tried to hire her for a season.

While in Naples, Emma also developed an art form she called "Attitudes" where she portrayed classical sculptures and paintings for an audience. Partly inspired by Romney's various paintings of her as classical figures, she used a variety of shawls to drape around her body, affecting different poses.

In the spring of 1787 Sir William unveiled his wife's new creation to rapturous response. The performances were described as almost like charades, with audience members shouting out guesses for which character Emma was portraying at a given time. [Figure 7] The German writer Goethe saw Emma perform and described it in glowing terms:

> She lets down her hair and, with a few shawls gives so much variety to her poses, gestures, expressions, etc. that the spectator can hardly believe his eyes. He sees what thousands of artists would have liked to express realized before him in movements and surprising transformations—standing,

> kneeling, sitting, reclining, serious, sad, playful, ecstatic, contrite, alluring, threatening, anxious. One pose follows another without a break. She knows how to arrange the fold of her veil to match each mood, and has a hundred ways of turning it into a headdress.[13]

Classical art was a major influence on the Regency period, and Emma helped solidify its hold. Historians often credit various women with popularizing classical dress at this time; Georgiana, Duchess of Devonshire, and Josephine, Empress of France, spring to mind. But Emma's engagement with classical inspiration was deeper. She attempted to enliven perhaps the most staid art form. She literally breathed life into sculptures.

All of this would be overshadowed by her most famous lover, the future Lord Nelson, who arrived in Naples on September 10, 1793. Emma, ambitious and eager to secure her place in history, maintained a correspondence with the famous general after he left.

The victorious Nelson returned to Naples in 1798. He'd lost an arm, most of his teeth, and was in generally poor health. Emma nursed him and even threw him a famous party to celebrate his fortieth birthday.

In 1799 Emma's power and importance in Nelson's life became clear as he attempted to end a revolution in Naples led by members of the aristocracy but unsupported by the common people. Emma acted as a go-between for Nelson and Queen Maria Carolina and helped to arrange the safe passage of the queen and her children back to Vienna.

Emma, Nelson, and Sir William traveled along with Emma's

mother back to England. Emma, who was now pregnant with Nelson's child, was introduced to Nelson's wife, Fanny Nisbet, for the first time.

Unlike Sir William, who accepted and even encouraged the affair, Fanny Nisbet was furious and humiliated by her husband's betrayal. She demanded that Nelson choose between her and Emma, and he did so, choosing Emma and taking steps to formalize a separation with Fanny.

Emma gave birth to their daughter Horatia on January 29, 1801. Emma and Nelson came up with a careful cover story for Horatia's birth, telling everyone that she was an orphan adopted from Naples. Nelson was abroad serving when the birth happened. He was also away in the immediate aftermath when Emma caught the eye of the Prince of Wales, leading to rumors about the two, and Sir William sending an extraordinary letter to his friend Nelson, assuring him that Emma had stayed faithful.

Nelson and Emma were both devoted parents who loved their daughter. One of Nelson's final wishes before his death was that Horatia take his last name, which she did. However, Emma continued the pretense that she was Horatia's "guardian" rather than mother until she died, and Horatia believed this.

Under Emma's direction, Nelson bought Merton Place and began to fix it up to her taste. The couple lived at Merton together with Sir William, Emma's mother, and a number of Nelson's relatives, much to the fascination of the British press.

Sir William died in Emma's arms in 1803, and his creditors soon descended. Emma was in a very difficult position. She couldn't and wouldn't remarry a rich man to obtain a fortune and clear the debts because she was so devoted to Nelson. Nelson's family had their own debts, and their requests for Emma's help—financially and/or socially—led to a strained relationship and complaints about her lack of generosity.

Soon after, Nelson left to fight in the Napoleonic Wars, leaving Emma pregnant with their second daughter, who sadly died just six weeks after her birth.

After a brief visit back to England in 1805, Nelson left again for the last time. He died on October 21, 1805, after being seriously injured in battle.

Nelson rewrote his will in the last days of his life, begging that Emma be provided with a pension in recognition for his service and, touchingly, that she sing at his funeral. He wished that Horatia would begin using his surname exclusively. He also left Emma a pension of his own, and their beloved home Merton.

Nelson's funeral was lavish, but Emma was excluded. Relations between her and Nelson's heir, his older brother William, became even more strained.

Eventually Emma's situation became so desperate that she put Merton up for sale in 1808, but it failed to sell at first. With the help of friends it eventually sold, but the proceeds only went so far. By 1812 Emma was so in debt that she was sentenced to time in jail, though she and Horatia were allowed to live in rooms outside the prison.

Emma's pleas for financial assistance to her many important friends like the Prince of Wales were ignored. She fled her debtors with Horatia to Calais in 1814 and died a year later. It was an ignominious death for such an important woman. After her mother's death Horatia refused to acknowledge her true parentage.

Emma's life was not a fairy tale, and there's no happy ending. She went from nothing to everything and nothing again.

She flipped the script whenever it suited her, marrying a man who planned for her to be a mistress and then turning around and becoming a mistress to an even more famous and powerful man.

In the annals of history, her work as a mistress has become inextricably linked with her art. The dismissal of her "Attitudes" seems to be directly tied to the shame historians think Emma should have for her relationships.

But Emma's life is marked by a seeming refusal to do what was expected of her, making her a fascinating example of a Mistress of the Regency.

LADY CAROLINE LAMB

"The cleverest, most agreeable, absurd, amiable, perplexing, dangerous, fascinating little being that lives now or ought to have lived 2000 years ago," wrote the poet George Byron, describing Lady Caroline Lamb.

She, in turn, described him as "mad, bad, and dangerous to know," and their affair lit up the Regency world with its scandalous intensity.

As the speaker of those words, Caroline is tied to the Regency and everything it stands for. But just like the era, her life has become blurred through years of fiction and historians intent on casting her in the singular role of hysterical, scorned lover.

The Honorable Caroline Ponsonby was born on November 13, 1785. Her mother, Henrietta, Countess of Bessborough, was the younger sister of Georgiana, Duchess of Devonshire. Her father, Frederick Ponsonby, became the third Earl of Bessborough upon his father's death. Henrietta and Frederick had a notoriously unhappy marriage, not unlike many of their contemporaries.

While Caroline was an only child, she was raised with a wide assortment of her legitimate and illegitimate cousins. She was extremely well educated under the watchful eye of her grandmother the Dowager Lady Spencer and developed a sharp writing style while attending school in London, where she was taught by noted poet Frances Arabella Rowden.

In 1805 Caroline married the Honorable William Lamb, heir to the first Viscount Melbourne. The pair were widely considered a love match. Caroline's cousin Harry described them as "mutually captivated."[14] After several miscarriages, they welcomed their first son in 1807, George Augustus Frederick. George was born with developmental disabilities, and Caroline and Frederick elected to keep him at home and school him rather than send him away as was the custom. In 1809 Caroline gave birth to a baby girl who only lived for a day.

While Caroline has the historical reputation for hysterics and bad behavior, William was certainly no saint. He had a well-known interest in whipping and administered beatings to his son, his serving girls, and his lovers after Caroline's death. There is no evidence that he whipped Caroline, but she once wrote that William's "violence is as bad as my own."[15]

No one expected Caroline and William to remain faithful to each other, given the goings-on and widespread infidelity in their social circle. But Caroline was incapable of keeping her love life private or even quiet, leading to anger and disgust from her family and social censure.

Her first affair was with well-known Regency playboy Sir Godfrey Vassal Webster. The pair spent the Season of 1810 showing their mutual affection far too publicly, leading William's mother to write and expose their tryst.

Caroline confessed the affair to William, who forgave her (much to his mother's dismay). But their relationship was damaged and, as Caroline wrote, "No time will ever bring me back the perfect innocence & enjoyment I once possessed nor shall I ever hear William's name or meet his eyes without feelings of bitter reproach."[16]

In 1811 Lord George Byron—profligate poet—returned to London after a trip abroad. He published his epic poem *Childe Harold's Pilgrimage* on March 3, 1812, and became a true celebrity overnight, courted by high society and the literary world alike.

Caroline wrote to Byron before they had even met, after she read an early copy of *Childe Harold*. "I have read your Book & cannot refrain from telling you that I think it & that all those whom I live with & whose opinions are far more worth having—think it beautiful. You deserve to be and shall be happy."[17]

The pair met at Holland House a few weeks later and embarked on an affair that would change the course of both of their lives.

While the aftermath of the affair was extremely dramatic, the time Byron and Caroline actually spent together sounds almost domestic. Byron visited Caroline at home, and spent time with her son Augustus. Byron and Caroline frequently exchanged gifts of books, always eager to hear what the other one thought.

Caroline had long had a penchant for dressing in men's clothing. She dressed as a page boy to visit Byron at his apartments without being seen. Byron, who experimented with his own sexuality at school, liked Caroline's flirting with such taboos.

Caroline is often charged with a singular obsession with Byron, and the impetus for the affair is put on her. But Byron was desperate to be accepted by exactly the social world Caroline had been born into. He was just as fascinated with her as she was with him. In April 1812 Byron wrote to Caroline, "Every word you utter, every line you write proves you to be either sincere or a fool, now as I know you are not the one I must believe you the other."[18] In Caroline, Byron had found a window into the Ton, and he fully exploited that.

But he went even a step further in courting and eventually marrying Caroline's cousin, Annabella Milbanke, finally actually ensuring his acceptance in high society. Caroline was actively involved in this courtship, passing letters and poems between the pair, perhaps her way of trying to maintain control.

But that was a façade. Byron was actually getting advice from Caroline's mother-in-law, Elizabeth Lamb, Lady Melbourne. She encouraged Byron to choose Annabella over Caroline. And that wasn't all Lady Melbourne did.

Despite her age of sixty, Lady Melbourne was still an attractive, compelling partner to Byron, who was always interested in older women. While Lady Melbourne's children destroyed any evidence of physical consummation of the relationship, their letters to each other are filled with flirtations. Byron relied on Lady Melbourne to help him end his affair with Caroline and marry her niece, Annabella Milbanke, writing, "You have been my director & are still for I do not know anything you could not make me do or undo."[19]

Caroline and Byron mutually engaged in various scandalous antics, like when Caroline sent Byron a clipping of her pubic hair. Several times they threatened to elope. Caroline's family, including both her mother and mother-in-law, were intimately involved in these episodes, writing to Byron to interfere and chasing Caroline down the street after she ran away.

To deal with her many emotions about the affair, Caroline turned to the solace she had always found in writing. She wrote a short story about a spaniel named Biondetta who is so devoted to Byron she dies when he spurns her. She ended the story with a quote from the poet William Cowper: "Attachment never to be wean'd or chang'd."[20]

In September 1812 Caroline, William, and her parents traveled to Ireland. Caroline's family hoped that distance would help bring a natural end to the affair. The pair exchanged letters, with Caroline's mother-in-law, Lady Melbourne, acting as a go-between and spy for Byron.

Upon her return to England, Caroline arranged an enormous public bonfire on which she burned Byron's letters and gifts to her. She also talked her way in to see Byron's publisher, John Murray, to steal a portrait of him, using a forged letter where she impersonated Byron to gain entry. This wouldn't be the first or the last time Murray acted as a go-between for the tempestuous lovers.

Caroline didn't just imitate Byron in private letters. She also began working in earnest on a response to his *Childe Harold*, secured a publisher, and received an advance of £100 for her manuscript.

Despite the distraction of work, the affair continued on as dramatic as ever as Byron tried to officially end the relationship. Stories differ, but one night at a waltzing party thrown by Lady Katherine Heathcote, there was a scene between the pair with Caroline brandishing a knife and possibly cutting herself.

Byron is frequently cast as desperate to end the relationship, but it's clear that Caroline remained an object of fascination for him long after his protestations to the contrary. In 1814 Byron finally got engaged to Annabella Milbanke. He insisted he be the one to tell Caroline, but when she arrived for their meeting he couldn't bring himself to tell the truth. Instead he told her about his incestuous relationship with his half sister Augusta and his dabbling in homosexual sex.

Caroline reacted calmly when she eventually found out the truth and wrote to Murray, "I trust in God Byron will be happy. He has chosen one who is good and amiable and who deserves well of him. It is his last chance of keeping clear of what has too often led him astray."[21]

Byron and Annabella's marriage was a disaster, and by February 1816 Annabella had left him. Caroline initially tried to help the couple reconcile, but after she heard the truth of their abusive marriage she took Annabella's side against Byron.

Around the same time, Caroline's mother- and sister-in-law had finally had enough of her antics, and redoubled their efforts to get William to leave Caroline by trying to have her declared insane. Lady Melbourne and Emily were unsuccessful and would come to regret that even more in the coming months.

On May 9, 1816, Caroline's first novel, *Glenarvon*, was published, anonymously at first. She was incredibly proud of her work, and wrote upon holding the finished novel in her hands, "[It] looks beautiful but made my heart beat!"[22]

Her heart may have beat because of the public and private furor coming her way.

Glenarvon is a Gothic romance set in Ireland and reads as high drama.

> Bright shone the stars that night, and to the imagination of the aged seer, it seemed in sleep, that the spirits of departed heroes and countrymen, freed from the bonds of mortality, were ascending in solemn grandeur before his eyes; Glenarvon's form appeared before him—his patron! his benefactor!—he spoke of times long past, of scenes by all forgot, pointed with a look of despondency to his infant son!—"Who shall protect the orphan that is destitute?"—he cried—"who shall restore him to the house of his fathers?"[23]

The heroine, Lady Calantha Delaval (a stand-in for Caroline herself), is the only daughter of the Duke and Duchess of Altamonte, set to inherit everything. Her scheming aunt Lady

Margaret Buchanan intends for her son and Calantha's cousin, William, to marry her and therefore inherit the Altamonte title.

Unfortunately for the dissolute Lady Margaret, the duchess conceives and gives birth to a new heir to the dukedom. Lady Margaret sends her lover Count Viviana to arrange for the child's murder, which he tells Lady Margaret he has done. The duchess dies of her grief. William, in his fury, refuses to marry Calantha, and his mother sends him to England hoping he'll change his mind.

Meanwhile Calantha is being cared for by another aunt, Mrs. Seymour. (Mrs. Seymour seems to be an amalgamation of the aunts and beloved grandmothers who raised Caroline, complete with two daughters who serve as confidantes and rivals to Caroline/Calantha.) Under her watch, Calantha falls in love with and marries Henry Mowbrey, the Earl of Avondale. (Avondale is a stand-in for Caroline's husband, William, described as "a noble mind and a warm uncorrupted heart."[24])

While Calantha loves her new husband, his family hates her. (And again, we see a clear connection to Caroline's own life and her complicated relationship with her in-laws.) Her husband, while loving, also mocks her for her naïveté and prudishness, and in her attempts to prove him wrong, Calantha enters into an affair with Irish rebel leader Glenarvon.

Glenarvon is secretly Clarence de Ruthven, the supposedly disappeared heir to the abbey at Belmont and the priory of St. Alvin. After leaving his former life, Ruthven has turned into Glenarvon, a ruthless seducer who induces erotomania in his victims, including

Calantha. (Erotomania is a rare delusional disorder in which the sufferer believes another individual is in love with them. By bringing it into her novel, Caroline seems to be poking at the accusations that she was the aggressor in her relationship with Byron, while he remained aloof and unfeeling.)

When Calantha finally dies, Lord Avondale challenges Glenarvon to a duel.

And here's where things really go off the rails: Glenarvon wounds Avondale, and then reveals that he, Glenarvon, is also Clarence de Ruthven *and* Count Viviana, Lady Margaret's disgraced lover.

He also reveals that the child was not actually killed, and in revealing this, tries to kill him once again. Failing, Glenarvon joins a British squadron but is tormented by visions of those whose lives he has ruined. He throws himself off the ship, and his fellow sailors pull him back, where he finally expires on the deck.

Glenarvon was widely considered a roman à clef in which a thin veil of fiction is pulled over real-life events, and the reader is left to decipher who is who by examining the relationship between fictional characters and real-life figures.

Lady Melbourne wrote to a friend about the novel, "I was so disgusted with the spirit in which it was written that after reading the first 20 pages, I declared I would read no more."[25]

Caroline was horrified and unprepared for the reaction from her nearest and dearest. She wrote to her sister-in-law Emily, "My Dearest Emily all I ask you is write to Lord & Lady M[elbourne] say to them I dare not ask them to forgive me... you will only let them know my heart is not quite hardened & I am miserable at having been so wicked."[26]

Caroline had one unwavering supporter: her husband William. He tried his best to smooth things over with offended family and friends, while also supporting Caroline as *Glenarvon* went into a second edition and as she worked on revisions for future editions.

The rest of their social circle was not so forgiving. Lady Jersey rescinded Caroline's voucher to Almack's, essentially barring her from the most important social event of the Season. Caroline's sister-in-law Emily was also a Patroness, and at William's urging she stepped in and talked Lady Jersey out of banning Caroline. "I have therefore fought a battle for her and put her name down to Almack's Balls in spite of Lady Jersey's Teeth—let people do as they like in their own private Society but I think it hard to exclude a person from a ball where six hundred people go if they really are received everywhere,"[27] wrote a clearly exasperated Emily.

Of course, in private, Emily continued to undermine Caroline's influence on William and pushed for their separation.

Caroline continued to publish her work, including the scathing Byronic satirical poem "A New Canto" (1819), and the novels *Graham Hamilton* (1822), *Ada Reis* (1823), and *Penruddock* (1823). She was an active and engaged writer, peppering her editor with letters and suggestions for how to improve her work and sales. She also befriended a number of important writers of the day, sending them her works-in-progress and asking for opinions, or offering her own on their most recent work. One such friend was Amelia Alderson Opie, who visited Caroline at her country home Brocket Hall, as did widowed husband of feminist Mary Wollstonecraft and father to the creator of Frankenstein Mary Shelley, William Godwin. She helped Godwin immeasurably with financial matters with her characteristic generosity.

In 1824 Byron died in Italy. Caroline was devastated and very focused on securing the return of the many letters she had sent to Byron from his friend Henry Hobhouse, who organized the burning of Byron's memoir.

Caroline was also struggling with her physical and mental health. She was now under the full-time care of two nurses, and when she became too overwrought they kept her locked away. A separation with William seemed inevitable, and Caroline's brother William began negotiating for a settlement on her behalf.

William was miserable at the proposed separation, but he was weakening in his resolve to stand up to his siblings. A deed of separation was drawn up, but both parties had to agree and sign and they both dragged their feet. Finally Caroline left for Paris, and then removed herself to her beloved Brocket Hall while William remained in London.

Caroline's health declined rapidly at the end of 1827 and on January 25, 1828, she died after a last visit with William and Augustus. The *Literary Gazette* printed a short biography of Caroline, which may have been written by William and which read in part, "Wild and impatient of restraint, rapid in impulses, generous, and kind of heart, —these were the first traits of her nature; and they continued to the last."[28]

CONCLUSION

> Let me ask the rational and thinking mortal, why the graces of feminine beauty are to be constituted emblems of a debilitated mind? Does the finest symmetry of form, or the most delicate tint of circulation, exemplify a tame submission to insult or oppression? Is the strength of intellect, in women, bestowed in vain? Has the SUPREME DISORDER OF EVENTS [sic] given to the female soul a distinguished portion of energy and feeling, that the one may remain inactive, and the other be the source of her destruction? Let the moralist think otherwise. Let the contemplative philosopher examine the proportions of human intellect; and let us hope that the immorality of the soul springs from causes that are not merely *sexual*.[29]

The words of Mary Robinson's *A Letter to the Women of England, on the Injustice of Mental Subordination* are just as poignant and relevant today as they were in the early nineteenth century. Contemporary feminists fight against and point out these exact same double standards that women face, especially if they commit the crime of being beautiful or sexual beings.

Mistresses fall into this trap all the time. They can also be infantilized and stripped of their agency for their sexual choices, or cast as the villain or the hysterical shrew, like Caroline Lamb. The pages of history are not an easy place for Mistresses.

The truth is far more subversive than historical perception.

These women didn't allow themselves to be defined by their relationships. They used their partners for monetary or social gain, even when and if there were real emotions involved.

Perhaps that is why Mistresses are so tricky to write about. They require us to wade into the realm of human emotion, something intangible and not at all black-and-white. While their relationships might have been transgressive, do we separate the art from the artist?

Mary Robinson, Grace Dalrymple Elliott, Emma Hamilton, and Lady Caroline Lamb certainly challenge us to. All the Mistresses of the Regency not included here do. We have to contend with them as women, artists, mothers, sisters, as complete pictures.

Recommended Reading

Andrews, Donna. "'Adultery à-la-Mode': Privilege, the Law and Attitudes to Adultery 1770–1809," *History* 82 (1997): 5–23.

Balogh, Mary. Mistress Series: *More than a Mistress* (2000), *No Man's Mistress* (2001), *The Secret Mistress* (2011). Avon.

Byrne, Paula. *Perdita: The Literary, Theatrical, Scandalous Life of Mary Robinson*. Random House, 2004.

Chase, Loretta. Fallen Women Series: *Your Scandalous Ways* (2008) and *Don't Tempt Me* (2009). Avon.

Douglass, Paul. *Lady Caroline Lamb: A Biography*. Palgrave Macmillan, 2016.

Manning, Jo. *My Lady Scandalous: The Amazing Life and Outrageous Times of Grace Dalrymple Elliott, Royal Courtesan*. Simon and Schuster, 2005.

Williams, Kate. *England's Mistress: The Infamous Life of Emma Hamilton*. Random House, 2009.

[Figure 5] *Florizel and Perdita*. Circa 1783.
Lewis Walpole Library.
(Courtesy of The Lewis Walpole Library, Yale University)

[Figure 6] George Romney.
Emma Hart as Circe. Circa 1782.
Tate Modern. *(©Tate, London 2019)*

[Figure 7] Pietro Antonio Novelli. *The Attitudes of Lady Hamilton.* After 1791. National Gallery of Art, Washington, DC. *(National Gallery of Art, Washington. Ailsa Mellon Bruce Fund.)*

CHAPTER FOUR

The Family Business

Artistic Families

When we consider the idea of networks, a very clear group emerges from the artists of the Regency. Both in fine art and on the stage, the same names appear again and again. That is because artistic families reigned supreme in Regency England, passing their craft down through the generations.

While there are any number of networks of women in the

Regency to discover, the network of female artists is unique for several reasons. First, they are literally connected by blood and marriage. These are networks brought together by genetics. But they also share their art. The successive generations of female artists grow these networks, so the women are building their careers in two very literal ways: through motherhood and through work. Having fought for their own careers and place in the art world, the artistic mothers of the Regency do not try to dissuade their daughters from following in their footsteps. Rather they encourage and facilitate their careers, often arranging for the highest level of private tutoring from artist friends, or teaching them themselves.

Networks of patronage are nothing new in the artistic world. But the strong maternal line in these Regency families is noteworthy. Here we see women passing their trade and talent on to the next generation. These family networks were useful for both consistency and growth. Many artists made their livings off commissions, and a familiar name helped secure customers. Daughters trained in simple tasks from a young age also made useful assistants, who could then try their hand at larger projects.

In these artistic family networks we are treated to a rare sight: ambitious women. Many of these artists helped to build their families' reputations and were keenly aware of their place in that mythos. This pride in successive generations can be seen in a number of ways, from private journals to commissioned paintings, like that of a young Fanny Kemble shortly after her stage debut and her much more famous and retired aunt Sarah Siddons. [Figure 8]

And these women were also forward thinking, aware that it

takes several generations to truly build a family legacy. To achieve their ambitions they carefully passed their craft on to their daughters, nieces, granddaughters, and daughters-in-law. In each successive generation the women had the opportunity to improve upon that which their foremothers taught them.

MOTHERS AND DAUGHTERS: THE SHARPLES AND THE BEETHAMS

At the end of the eighteenth century and into the early nineteenth we are presented with two fascinating examples of mothers and daughters who worked together and separately building successful careers as professional and critically respected artists, across generations.

Ellen Sharples married her art teacher and raised two children with him, both of whom became artists. Ellen trained her daughter Rolinda herself, recording the process in her diaries. She was thrilled when her daughter's talent surpassed her own and Rolinda began taking on more ambitious projects, including one of the paintings more closely visually associated with the Regency period, *The Cloakroom, Clifton Assembly Rooms* (1817–1818). [Figure 9]

Isabella Beetham is considered one of the greatest silhouette artists of her time. She founded her own studio on Fleet Street in London where she made her much-sought-after portraits. Isabella's eldest daughter, Jane, began working for her mother in the 1790s. She quickly developed her own style, and as with Rolinda Sharples her ambition exceeded her mother's. While her marriage curbed her career for a short while, she reappeared in the professional art world in 1805 and exhibited at the Academy until her death in 1815.

THE SHARPLES

Already established as a successful artist, John Sharples married his pupil Ellen Wallace in 1787, shortly after the birth of their first son, James, in 1785. Not much is known of Ellen's early life, except that she lived in Bath and was raised Quaker. Her husband and his family were Catholic but it doesn't seem to have been a problem for the new couple. They were married in St. Mary's Church, a Church of England parish church. John had two sons from two previous marriages, George and Felix, and in 1793 daughter Rolinda joined the family. Shortly thereafter they packed up and moved to America.

Along the way, their ship was captured by French pirates, and the family was imprisoned in France for several months before gaining their release. Ellen wrote about the ordeal in her diary: "War! how dreadful the sound, whichever way contemplated misery precedes, accompanies, and follows in its train. Our family have experienced; severely experienced much of its misery, and much did we witness during our seven months captivity in France, too heart rending to red [sic]."[1]

They arrived in New York in 1796 and set up shop as portraitists to the founding fathers and mothers of America. John quickly rose to prominence after painting George Washington. Ellen, and the rest of the family, acted as copyists and assistants to John while also painting themselves. This included their daughter Rolinda, who was educated alongside her brothers and a full member of the family business. Ellen in particular took an interest in her daughter's education, keeping a careful record of Rolinda's steady improvement in her journal:

> It is very delightful to me to see her always cheerful and happy, ardently engaged in various intellectual pursuits, particularly that of painting, for which she has a decided taste. Exercising it as a profession she views as attended with every kind of advantage. The employment itself is a positive pleasure; It procures in exchange many articles of utility & luxury that otherwise wd be regarded as extravagance the persons she draws entertain her whilst sitting, become her friends and continue to be so, ever after meeting her with smiling countenances and kind greetings, and invarious [sic] ways show her attention, and contribute to her amusement.[2]

Around 1800 the family returned to England, and Ellen began encouraging Rolinda in earnest, paying her small amounts to complete drawings. It's important to note that Ellen instilled an entrepreneurial spirit in her daughter, at least in regard to her art. Rolinda learned early that art could produce income.

Rolinda's talent surpassed that of both her parents and her brothers. As Ellen pointed out, Rolinda was "pursuing her profession with the greatest ardour, most desirous to attain excellence."[3] She worked at her painting every day. Like many other artists, Rolinda painted portraits on commission, which was her bread and butter. Many of her friends and social circle sat for her. But she also tackled larger, more prestigious projects like large-scale group scenes and history paintings. She displayed at the Royal Academy in 1820, 1822, and 1824. Paintings hung at the Royal Academy had to be submitted, and it was extremely prestigious to be chosen. Few women received the honor. Rolinda's paintings were critically well received, and in 1827 she was unanimously elected a member of the newly formed Society of British Artists, the highest honor bestowed on a female artist.

Rolinda's painting *The Cloakroom, Clifton Assembly Rooms* (1817–1818) is one of the most enduringly iconic images of the Regency. She captured the crowd preparing for an evening, flirting and bowing and fixing their shoes. Unlike so many of the famous caricatures of this period, Rolinda has rendered the crowd with warmth and grace. It's also important that Rolinda portrayed a wide range of ages and characters, including the servants integral to the aristocratic Regency way of life. Perhaps her unique position as a female artist, and one who had traveled so widely and seen so much, encouraged her to shine a light on everyone in the scene rather than those we usually see.

This warmth can also be seen in her self-portrait with her mother, painted in 1816. [Figure 10] Rolinda sits at an easel, wearing a fashionable if impractical white dress, her hands full of the tools of her trade: brushes and a leather stick she used to keep her hand off the paint. Her mother, Ellen, stands next to her, dressed in black, leaning over to look at the painting her daughter is working on. While Rolinda looks at the viewer with a gentle expression, her mother views her work. We're reminded of the maternal pride she must feel in her daughter's accomplishments. We're also, in no uncertain terms, told who taught Rolinda. Ellen is given the privileged position of a revered teacher.

John and Ellen traveled back to America in 1809 to continue building their business, but tragedy struck the family when John died in 1811. Ellen chose to return to Bristol with Rolinda, while George and Felix stayed in America.

Rolinda was elected an honorary member of the Society of British Artists in 1827 in recognition of her talent and impressive career. She lived with her mother at the end of her life, and died from breast cancer in 1838.

Ellen experienced one tragedy after another, losing first her beloved daughter and then her son James just a year later to pneumonia. She spent her final years helping to establish the Bristol Academy for the Promotion of Fine Art. When she died in 1849 she left her considerable estate to the academy.

Included in that estate were the meticulous journals that Ellen kept throughout much of her life. The journals provide us an intimate look at the daily life of a family of artists in the nineteenth century. Unlike some other journals or diaries, these were written for personal use, not with an eye for publication. They include many personal musings on the health and happiness of Ellen's family including her husband, her sons, and her daughter. Ellen carefully copied earlier journals, letters, and other miscellaneous papers into new journals, as well as including excerpts from Rolinda's own journals.

In 1814 the family visited London and Ellen wrote about attending the Royal Exhibition with Rolinda and James, then in their early twenties. "The pleasure with which James & Rolinda viewed the pictures, and the advantage they would probably derive from attentively observing them, gave me an additional interest to seek out the various beauties in the works of the most distinguished artists."[4]

Intergenerational careers are nothing new. But rarely do we have such an intact record of the internal feelings of both a mother and a daughter as they embark upon and achieve successful careers as artists in the nineteenth century.

Ellen was proud of Rolinda. She writes as much and often in her journals and she took special care to preserve Rolinda's own journals and correspondence after her untimely death.

But Rolinda was also proud of Ellen. It's clear in her self-portrait as, in the place of honor where a beloved teacher and mentor might stand, she has painted her mother, the woman who taught her to paint and to dream about where her painting might take her.

THE BEETHAM/READS

Isabella Beetham, née Robinson, was born circa 1754. Isabella's family was Catholic, royalist, and firmly well off. Little is known of her upbringing or education, but her grandfather was an architect so perhaps art and design were included.

In early 1773 Isabella met and eloped with Edward Beetham. That year also saw the addition of the couple's first daughter, Jane, who would be followed by five more siblings.

As if the elopement wasn't scandalous enough, the two had also decided to pursue artistic professions. Edward worked as an actor at Sadler's Wells and Haymarket Theatres in London. He also invented a curtain for the front of the stage that rolled up, minimizing the risk of it catching on fire. Unfortunately, Edward was not in a position to patent the invention so he didn't receive the bulk of the profits. But he was undeterred and continued inventing, eventually landing on a new kind of washing machine that used wooden rollers to wring excess water out of fabric.

Meanwhile, Isabella embarked on an artistic career. While she initially started with the traditional method of cutting silhouettes, after she studied with successful miniature portraitist John Smart, her work became far more complicated as she mastered the art of painting, a new method for creating the coveted profiles.

Edward and Isabella supported their growing family jointly. In 1785 the family established themselves at 27 Fleet Street where they lived and sold Edward's washing machines. Isabella set up a studio on the upper floor where she worked on her silhouettes. This involved a painstaking and intensive process of painting directly on glass. Isabella was successful enough to employ at least two assistants, along with help from her daughter Jane. She also took out advertisements to bring in new customers.

> Mrs. BEETHAM, who has ever been distinguished as one of the most eminent who ever attempted PROFILE LIKENESSES, continues to execute them with that Taste and Elegance which remains unrivalled. She paints them on Chrystals, ornamented with gold and silver, displaying the hair and drapery in a manner more beautiful than can be

> conceived till seen: and if not the most striking likeness, no gratuity will be expected. She likewise finishes them on IVORY, COMPOSITION, AND PAPER, for RINGS, LOCKETS, BRACELETS, &c.
>
> Time of Sitting, One Minute.[5]

She wasn't exaggerating. Isabella was one of the most famous silhouette artists of her time. She had a distinct style and a unique talent for rendering details like hair and lace with hatching and crosshatching that was widely sought after.

Like Ellen Sharples, Isabella seems to have passed on everything she knew to her daughter. She also arranged for Jane to receive tutelage from close family friend and celebrated painter John Opie. Opie was a good teacher, and Jane had clearly inherited natural talent from her mother. She exhibited for the first time at the Academy in 1794, when she was just twenty years old.

John Opie's first marriage was an unhappy one, and his close relationship to his student Jane seems to have caused a bit of gossip in the close-knit artistic community in London. After Opie divorced his wife in 1796 he quickly asked Edward for Jane's hand in marriage, but was roundly rejected.

SPOTLIGHT ON AMELIA ALDERSON OPIE

John Opie didn't remain single after being rejected by Jane Beetham. He fell in love at first sight with Amelia Alderson at a party in Norwich sometime in 1797.

Amelia Alderson is a fascinating figure in her own right, irrespective of her marriage.

Born on November 12, 1769, to wealthy Norwich doctor James Alderson and his wife, Amelia Briggs, Amelia was raised in a liberal household. Her mother passed away in 1784, and Amelia took over the duties of housekeeper and hostess. She became friends with many leading liberal thinkers of the day including William Godwin, who nursed a crush on her, and his eventual wife Mary Wollstonecraft, one of the most famous feminists of all time, author of *A Vindication of the Rights of Woman* (1792).

Amelia initially resisted John Opie's charms and marriage proposals. Finally, after he assured her that her father would be welcome to live with them in their marital home, she assented. The pair were married in 1798.

Despite her initial misgivings, the marriage proved to be a happy one. Opie's art certainly benefited, as he began to receive critical praise for his paintings of women. At least one contemporary attributed the positive change to Opie's marriage to Amelia.

Amelia's artistic career also flourished after her marriage. With Opie's encouragement she published her first acknowledged novel in 1801, *Father and Daughter.*[6] The year after, she published a collection of poetry so popular it went through six editions. She followed this with another collection of poetry, and then thirteen more novels.

In 1807 John Opie died. Amelia retreated to Norwich and channeled her grief into working on a memoir about him, which was published in 1809.

She returned to London and her former social life in 1810. Ten years later she left once more for Norwich, to nurse her ailing father. He passed away in 1825, and Amelia turned for comfort to Quaker friends—a religion she was familiar with due to her friendship with the Gurney family, old neighbors from Norwich.

Amelia's official conversion to become a Quaker caused a stir among her old circle in London. But she was committed deeply to the religion and especially its connection to the abolition movement. Amelia did not allow her new religion to impede her lifestyle. She continued to travel, especially to Paris where she met Queen Marie Amélie and Georges Cuvier. She did, however, cease publishing fiction, as it was frowned upon by Quakers.

In 1840 Amelia attended the first World Anti-Slavery Convention and was important enough to be one of several women included in Benjamin Robert Haydon's painting *The Anti-Slavery Society Convention*, painted a year later. [Figure 11]

Women, such as Amelia, were not officially invited to the convention, much to their consternation, but many showed up anyway. Much of the first day was spent discussing their inclusion. Eventually they were allowed to sit in the balcony and watch the proceedings, but not allowed to speak. Attendees Lucretia Mott and Elizabeth Cady Stanton were so incensed by their exclusion that they went home and organized their own convention, the Seneca Falls Convention, where they, in turn, excluded Black women from attending.

(BACK TO JANE BEETHAM)

Jane married a solicitor, John Read, soon after Opie's failed proposal. And she stopped exhibiting for several years.

This has led to speculation that she was in love with John Opie, that her marriage was an unhappy one, and that one or both of these things contributed to her break from her public career. We have no concrete evidence indicating anything of the sort, and Jane returned to exhibiting in 1805, continuing to do so until 1815.

Jane and John Read had one daughter, Cordelia. Jane and Cordelia lived together after John's death. Cordelia appears to have never married, and it's thanks to her slight hoarding tendencies that we have so much of her mother's art still extant.

Upon her death, Cordelia left her collection of her family's paintings and £100,000 to the Brompton Consumption Hospital. The paintings were in poor condition and many needed restoration, but Cordelia still ensured that the legacy of the artistic women in her family remained intact.

ANNE MEE

Born circa 1775 to John Foldsone and Elizabeth Fell, Anne was the oldest of eight children. Educated at Madam Pommier's in Bloomsbury, Anne felt the heavy weight of supporting her family on her shoulders in 1787 when her father passed away.

Luckily, John had been a miniaturist of middling talent, and his daughter had inherited all of it and then some. She began painting in earnest and received royal patronage and recognition, painting many of the leading society ladies. She even received a commission from the notoriously picky Horace Walpole, who then complained bitterly in subsequent letters when she was late delivering the paintings.

In 1793 Anne married Joseph Mee, an Irish barrister with an estate in Armagh. They had eight children between 1795 and 1807. Anne continued her painting career under her married name, Mrs. Joseph Mee. She appears to have only painted women, but whether this was due to her husband's purported jealousy or simply coincidence is unknown.

Anne displayed at the Royal Academy, indicating the technical proficiency of her miniatures. She was also a frequent visitor in court after 1790, when she drew Queen Charlotte. George IV, as Prince Regent, commissioned Anne to paint miniatures of the leading beauties at court, which she eventually published in 1812 as *Gallery of Beauties of the Court of George III.* She included her own portrait at the front.

Gallery of Beauties references past similar projects, like Peter Lely's *Windsor Beauties* from the mid-1660s. These series of portraits captured the favored and famous beauties in aristocratic circles. Many of Anne's beauties are depicted as Greek goddesses or other classical beauties, complete with gauzy veils and blowing hair.

As painter for this project, Anne joined an important lineage of formerly all-male artists asked to codify the women approved by royal choice. George IV, a notorious womanizer and lover of women, commissioned the project and wanted some record of the women at his father's court. It was an expansive project, with

Anne painting over eighteen full-size oil portraits of women such as Georgiana Augusta Frederica Seymour, the daughter of Grace Dalrymple Elliott, and possibly George IV himself.

Joseph died in 1849 and left his estate in Armagh to Anne, with bequests to their three sons. Anne wrote her will in 1850, leaving everything to her son Arthur Patrick, an architect who had followed in his mother's footsteps and exhibited at the Royal Academy. She died a year later in 1851.

THE ACTRESSES

Actresses are one of those groups that have gotten a truly terrible, all-encompassing reputation over the years, accumulated from rumor and innuendo. But many actresses in the early nineteenth century were firmly a part of the middle class, achieving financial and critical success in a way that was rare for women of the time.

That is not to absolve the profession of its more scandalous associations entirely. A number of high-profile mistresses trod the boards before, after, and during their assignations with royalty and aristocrats. Indeed, several of them were so successful in their amatory pursuits that their paramours married them. These marriages had varying levels of success in social settings, particularly depending on the birth of the actress in question.

The nineteenth century saw the founding of a number of famous theatrical families, the most famous of which is the Kembles. Much like the artistic families described above, these theatrical families passed their talents down through the generations, supporting their successors whenever possible. There was an added difficulty encouraging young women to pursue careers in the theater, especially if parents wanted their daughters to make respectable marriages, but ambitious young actresses found unique ways around this and managed to continue their family legacies.

Sarah Siddons and the Kembles

No actress was more famous during the Regency than Sarah Siddons. Her talent was unmatched, and her powerful family helped cement her place on the stage, where she ruled the Regency theater scene. Sarah Siddons was a celebrity and an it-girl long before the term was even in popular use.

Born on July 5, 1755, to the actor and theater manager Roger Kemble and his wife, Sarah Ward, Sarah was the first of twelve children. Seven of the twelve became actors, with varying degrees of success.

Sarah was initially educated on the road traveling with her parents, but eventually attended Mrs. Harris's School for Young Ladies where she felt out of place due to her lowborn status—which she quickly made up for by displaying her acting talents in school plays. At the same time she appeared in her family's theatrical performances. Her first recorded performance was in 1766 as Ariel in *The Tempest.*

Sarah's career was self-chosen and -directed. Her parents opposed her entering their profession and encouraged her to marry a local squire. Despite this, Sarah fell in love with fellow actor William Siddons. To discourage the relationship (and possible future profession) Sarah's parents sent her to work for Lady Mary

Greatheed at Guy's Cliffe, Warwick, where she was first a lady's maid and then a companion to Lady Mary.

Sarah and William continued to communicate and in 1773 her parents finally relented and the couple were married. They joined the Kembles' company for a year and then traveled to Cheltenham, where Sarah's performances started receiving particular attention.

Multiple people informed the famous David Garrick of Sarah's talents, but it wasn't until 1775 that he engaged her to perform with his Drury Lane company. Sarah was pregnant with her second child at the time, but she didn't let that slow her down, continuing to rehearse while pregnant. Her daughter was born November 4 and Sarah was already in London and performing on December 29 as Portia in *The Merchant of Venice.*

This debut was a disaster. Her performance was widely panned by critics and theatergoers alike.

Sarah retreated to Birmingham for the summer season, where she was informed that Garrick wouldn't be reengaging her contract. Devastated but determined to continue building her career, she spent six long years doing just that in theaters outside London.

In 1778 Sarah was engaged to perform at the Theatre Royal in Bath. Bath had become an increasingly popular and important vacation spot, and it was here that Sarah began to finally reclaim her reputation as an actress. Here she also befriended a number of important aristocratic women—including Georgiana, Duchess of Devonshire, and Fanny Burney—who would become important champions for her work.

After years of working on her craft, Sarah finally returned to the London stage on October 10, 1782, in the title role of *Isabella, or, The Fatal Marriage.*

The response could not have been more different from her disastrous debut. She was met with rapturous reviews and a number of articles detailing the wild, emotional reaction she elicited in her audiences, especially women. There were "sobs and shrieks . . . literally the spectators were too ill to use their hands in her applause."[7] One woman had to be carried out. Or as Byron said simply, "Nothing ever was or can be like her."[8]

In 1783 Sarah was invited to perform in front of the king and queen, and the queen appointed her official reader to the princesses. This level of royal approval was reflected in Sarah's continuing professional success. Her picture was painted by leading artists of the day, including Sir Joshua Reynolds, and engravings were published in every newspaper. In short, Sarah Siddons had become a star.

Unfortunately, Sarah's personal life was much more complicated. Her husband, William Siddons, was an alcoholic and terrible money manager. His own acting career had long been eclipsed by his wife's, which led to great resentment. William was also unfaithful, and Sarah believed that her ill health for much of her later life was due to a venereal disease he gave her.

Sarah's daughters, Sally and Maria, also enacted their own drama, which took an additional toll on their mother's health, in the late 1790s as they went back and forth over the painter Thomas Lawrence who first proposed to Sally in 1796 and then transferred his affections to the younger sister, Maria, when Sarah and William Siddons opposed the first match. Thomas Lawrence and Maria were engaged, against parental inclinations, in 1781. Maria's health began to deteriorate soon after the engagement, and Thomas went back to Sally. On her deathbed Maria made Sally promise not to enter a relationship with Thomas after her death, which she faithfully saw out. Sadly, Sally died five short years after Maria. The loss of her beloved daughters left Sarah's mental and physical health in shambles.

As a famous member of a famous family, Sarah was at the heart of the in-real-life drama surrounding the English theatrical world of the nineteenth century. Her career was at the whim of jealous and competitive theater managers, who played her against her competitors, trying to ensure that their theater had the best actress for the cheapest price.

Sarah and William Siddons maintained the careful veil of a happy marriage until 1804, when they informally separated. This was only after years of rumors surrounding Sarah and her former fencing instructor Mr. P. Galindo, resulting in Mrs. Galindo publishing her accusations against the couple in 1809. Sarah's role as a faithful wife and devoted mother was absolutely integral to her meteoric rise and eventual rule of the British stage, and any hint of impropriety could seriously damage that image. Unlike many of her contemporary actresses, Sarah was not a scandalous figure (at least for the better part of her career), as best seen in her connections to the royal family and especially the princesses, who were known to be extremely sheltered and protected by their royal parents. Luckily for Sarah, the Galindo episode, while unpleasant, didn't affect her celebrity status.

Sarah played her final season at Covent Garden in 1811–12. Her final performance as Lady Macbeth led to a stunning moment when the audience refused to allow the performance to continue after the sleepwalking scene, demanding Sarah's return to the stage. She did so in her own clothes, addressing the crowd in an emotional eight-minute speech.

Sarah maintained her retirement, except for the occasional benefit or family performance. She died on June 8, 1831.

Fanny Kemble

Born on November 29, 1809, to Sarah Siddons's brother Charles Kemble and his Viennese-born wife, Marie Thérèse de Camp, Fanny was the daughter, and niece, of noted actors. As such she received an enviable education in the arts, even studying in Paris for a time.

Fanny first appeared on the London stage as Juliet in *Romeo and Juliet* in 1829. The London *Times* wrote in a review, "Upon the whole, we do not remember to have ever seen a more triumphant debut. That Miss Kemble has been well and carefully instructed, as, of course, she would be is clear; but it is no less clear that she possesses qualifications which instructions could not create, although it can bring them to perfection."[9]

After her triumphant debut, Fanny toured around Great Britain, receiving accolades for her performances and securing her position as a leading actress of the time. Soon after she left for a planned two-year theatrical tour of the United States, accompanied by her father and her aunt Dall. While on tour Fanny attracted the attention and affections of Pierce Butler, heir to a number of plantations and scion of an important American family.

Fanny and Pierce were married in 1834 in Philadelphia. The couple had two daughters, Sarah and Frances. Upon their wedding, Fanny retired from her stage career. However, she wanted to continue to write, which her husband strongly discouraged.

While Pierce had courted Fanny assiduously, he treated her very differently after their marriage. He expected her to put aside her past life and everything associated with it and become a perfect society matron. Fanny rebelled against these expectations every way she could.

She published her private journals in 1835, against her husband's wishes and much to his horror and embarrassment. *A Journal of America* was an instant bestseller. Her family in England was distressed at the scandal, but no one was more distraught than Pierce Butler. The couple continued to fight, and Fanny even ran away several times.

In 1838 Fanny made her first trip to the plantation her husband had inherited on St. Simon's Island. She wrote her observations of the trip in a series of letters that she eventually published in 1863, once again over her husband's objections. In her diary Fanny paints a horrible picture, but she's quick to point out she's simply telling the truth: "I do not wish to add to, or perhaps I ought to say take away from, the effect of such narration by amplifying the simple horror and misery of their bare details."[10]

Slavery was the defining issue of Fanny and Pierce's marriage. They both thought they could convince the other of the rightness of their position, but neither budged. Their daughters split between them, with Sarah siding with her mother and Frances siding with her father.

The marriage was damaged irrevocably by the visit and Fanny left for England without her daughters in 1845. To support herself, she returned to the stage for a successful career as a reader of Shakespeare's plays.

In 1849 Pierce sued Fanny for divorce, with him retaining custody of their daughters. He also published a rebuttal to what he saw as her lies, 188 pages called *Mr. Butler's Statement*, in which he laid out why he and Fanny divorced, blaming the fact that "she held that marriage should be companionship on equal terms."[11] He also recklessly gambled and spent his massive fortune, leading to financial ruin. In 1859 his slaves were sold in what was the single largest slave auction in US history. He died in 1867.

In her later years Fanny settled back in England with her daughter Frances and her family. She published a series of memoirs starting in 1878, which provide historians an inside look at the theatrical world of the nineteenth century. She also paid careful attention to her ex-husband's business dealings, always with an eye to protecting her daughters and ensuring their futures.

CONCLUSION

In her Capital Theater Series (*Somewhere I'll Find You* and *Because You're Mine*) Lisa Kleypas harnesses all the drama and intrigue of the Regency theater world.

In *Somewhere I'll Find You*, the heroine Julia Wentworth ran away from her arranged marriage to follow her passion for the stage. But her fiancé shows up, determined to end their engagement and free himself, before he quickly falls in love with her. Julia's fiancé is Damon Savage, the Duke of Leeds, and while the pair fight about Julia's determination to continue her career after their marriage, they eventually come to an agreement. Julia continues as a director and actress even after she becomes a duchess.

In *Because You're Mine*, Miss Madeline Matthews is also trying to escape an arranged marriage, and decides the best way to do that is to ruin her reputation by sleeping with leading actor Logan Scott. Unfortunately, her plan goes awry and Madeline and Logan end up married to each other, trying to figure out how they fit into each other's worlds.

Both books bring us into the intimate, chaotic world of Regency theaters, full of characters like chatty dressers, ambitious aspiring actresses, clever set designers, and domineering directors—all of whom we could easily find real-life counterparts to in the pages of history. While Julia and Madeline are both running away from their families, and therefore devoid of a familial network to help with their careers, they find community within the theater. Both make friends with other aspiring actresses and actors while finding their way, including with each other. Julia even helps Madeline find housing with her old friend Nell Florence, a long-retired actress.

Through these different generations of actresses, Kleypas draws on the very real history of the Regency theater world to show the difficulties and the joys of life as an actress in the early nineteenth century.

Regency romance novels have also plumbed the depths of the art world, finding inspiration in the female artists of the Regency, like *River of Fire* by Mary Jo Putney, with heroine Rebecca Seaton who is not only an artist herself, but also the daughter of famous artist Sir Anthony Seaton. Or Sophia Hathaway from Tessa Dare's *Surrender of a Siren*, who leaves her life and advantageous marriage behind to secure the life she wants, as an artist.

These artists, much like the actresses from Kleypas's books, are drawn to art from somewhere deep within. It's innate in their character that they are artists who create.

In the words and art of the real female artists of the Regency we see this same passion and drive. And in the consecutive generations we see the fires of that passion fanned until each woman gets a chance to set the Regency world ablaze with her art.

Recommended Reading

Borzello, Frances. *A World of Our Own: Women as Artists Since the Renaissance.* Watson-Guptill Publications, 2000.

Clinton, Catherine. *Fanny Kemble's Civil Wars.* Oxford University Press, 2001.

Dare, Tessa. *Surrender of a Siren.* Avon, 2009.

Hayes, Joy. "Shady Ladies: Female Silhouette Artists of the 18th Century." *Antiques Journal*, June 2009: 26–29.

Kleypas, Lisa. *Somewhere I'll Find You.* Avon, 1996.

Kleypas, Lisa. *Because You're Mine.* Avon, 1997.

Nussbaum, Felicity. *Rival Queens: Actresses, Performance, and the Eighteenth-Century British Theater.* University of Pennsylvania Press, 2010.

Putney, Mary Jo. *River of Fire.* Signet, 1996.

Richards, Sandra. *Rise of the English Actress.* Palgrave Macmillan, 1993.

[Figure 8] Henry Perronet Briggs (circa 1791/93–1844).
Fanny Kemble and Her Aunt, Mrs. Siddons, circa 1830–31.
(Boston Athenaeum)

[Figure 9] Rolinda Sharples.
The Cloakroom, Clifton Assembly Rooms. 1817.
(The Cloakroom, Clifton Assembly Rooms [oil on canvas], Sharples, Rolinda [1794–1838]/Bristol Museum and Art Gallery, UK/Purchased, 1931./Bridgeman Image.)

[Figure 10] *Self-portrait of Rolinda Sharples with her mother Ellen Sharples.* 1820.
(The Artist and Her Mother [oil on panel], Sharples, Rolinda [1794–1838]/ Bristol Museum and Art Gallery, UK/Purchased, 1931./Bridgeman Images.)

[Figure 11] Benjamin Robert Haydon. *The Anti-Slavery Society Convention, 1840*. 1841.
(© National Portrait Gallery, London)

CHAPTER FIVE

Our STEM Foremothers

There has been a recent spate of romance novels set during the Regency time period featuring heroines engaged in scientific research. Heroines like the delightful Miss Madeline Gracechurch of Tessa Dare's *When a Scot Ties the Knot*, who spends much of the novel wrangling the pair of lobsters she is supposed to be observing for scientific purposes. Or Cara Elliott's Circle of Sin Series, which centers on a group of female friends pursuing intellectual careers in the sciences. Sometimes people chuckle when I recommend such a novel to them in my bookstore, the Ripped Bodice. They laugh because romance novels are considered the ultimate fantasy and even there, they cannot imagine a female scientist in the nineteenth century.

Not only did women work in the scientific communities of the nineteenth century, but many of them worked together, supporting each other's work, creating yet another example of an in-real-life network of Regency women.

There are some major names that emerge over and over in discussion of women and science during the nineteenth century—Caroline Herschel, Mary Anning, Jane Marcet, and Mary Somerville. Each, in her own way, has become a part of the storybook version of history. And they've each been put into a little box, rarely to be reexamined: Caroline Herschel as the devoted assistant to her brother, Mary Anning as the little old lady selling seashells, Jane Marcet as the consummate teacher, and Mary Somerville as the "queen of science."

These boxes separate the women from one another, holding each one out as an unusual oddity rather than a part of a much larger cohesive community.

Making your way as a woman in the scientific communities of the nineteenth century was not an easy task. These women had to battle prejudice and constant questioning and undermining of their talents and motives.

The women in this chapter succeeded in achieving their dreams. They received recognition in their lifetimes—some more than others. But more important they left behind a record for historians to find, evidence of their work and lives. As we sift through their words and stories we see tantalizing glimpses of other women working in and around science. These assistants, observers, and helpers deserve recognition and study.

No matter whether they were celebrated or unseen and unthanked in their own time, the scientific-minded women of the Regency made incredible advancements in their fields.

CAROLINE HERSCHEL

Caroline Herschel is often credited as the first woman to discover a comet. It won't surprise anyone reading this book to know that that honor actually goes to another woman, Maria Kirch, whose discovery of a previously unknown comet in 1702 was initially attributed to her husband and who spent her entire life fighting for any shred of official validation for her work in astronomy.

Caroline avoided a similar fate with her careful insertion of herself into her brother's work and the greater scientific community. She also made sure her legacy was secure by writing two autobiographies, as well as a final memoir that she never finished. Instead she cheekily suggested that her niece Arabella continue the story, as a novel. That never happened. But what I wouldn't give to read it!

Despite the pains Caroline took to write her own story, her autonomy as an astronomer has been very much called into question by historians. Her importance has become intertwined with her famous brother, William Herschel, a fellow astronomer. Due to the complicated relationship between the siblings, historians have chosen to simplify Caroline into a devoted servant and apprentice to her brother, stripping her of her own ambition. Although Caroline may have couched her motivations in acceptable language for the nineteenth century, she worked hard and wanted recognition for that work.

Caroline was born in Hanover, Germany, in 1750. She was the eighth child and fourth daughter in a not particularly wealthy or noble family. Her father, Isaac, was an oboist who became bandmaster of the Hanoverian Foot Guards. History tells us that her father supported his daughter's education while her mother decidedly did not. The truth, of course, is slightly more complicated. While Isaac Herschel was born to a gardener and the daughter of a tanner, he had clear ambition. He taught himself the oboe and rose in the ranks of the guards. His wife, Anna Ilse Moritzen, was born to a provincial family near Hanover. Her upbringing must have been very different from her husband's, and as such, history tells us that she lacked the ambition he had.

But because of the brilliant Caroline, we are given the chance to reexamine both mother and daughter centuries later. Caroline's memories of her mother are not happy ones. In her memoirs, she tells stories of being forgotten and overlooked by her mother. And perhaps more important, it was Anna who insisted Caroline end her formal education in favor of learning embroidery and other useful household tasks.

Caroline also lived with a physical disfigurement, from a childhood bout of smallpox. Both her mother and father seem to have been in agreement that it meant there was little chance of their daughter contracting an advantageous marriage.

Caroline seemed to associate all the bad memories of her childhood with her mother, while she remembered her father with great affection and admiration. In particular she remembered his excitement at sharing the eclipse in April 1764 with his children. He gathered them around a tub of water in the courtyard so they could safely view the phenomenon in the reflection. Caroline remembered him urging his children to look to the stars and consider the heavens.

Anna, on the other hand, wanted Caroline to stay at home and serve as the family's maid. In Caroline's memoirs she reflects on this, and offhandedly mentions that Anna believed if her sons hadn't become so educated they wouldn't have left Hanover and their family for England, which they did in 1766. A year later Isaac passed away, and Anna was left a widow with many children to take care of.

Perhaps Anna simply wanted what was left of her family to stay together.

It was not to be. Caroline escaped her life in Hanover in 1772, when she moved to Bath, England, at the invitation of her brother William.

William had settled in Bath as an organist and music teacher, and invited his sister to join him. While Caroline had played the violin a bit as a child, she was not a trained musician. But she clearly recognized the opportunity for what it was, and spent hours training her voice, as well as preparing her family in Hanover for her absence.

When Caroline arrived in England in 1772, she didn't speak English. Her brothers gave her a six-week crash course, and then sent her off by herself to the market.

Indeed, all the household tasks once again seemed to fall on Caroline, despite her burgeoning musical career and the hopes she had for it. Caroline struggled in her new life, and wrote in her memoirs, "The three winter months passed on very heavily. I had to struggle against *heimwehe* (home sickness) and low spirits, and to answer my sister's melancholy letters on the death of her husband, by which she became a widow with six children. I knew too little English to derive any consolation from the society of those who were about me, so that, dinner-time excepted, I was entirely left to myself."[1]

And then everything changed again.

William had become increasingly interested in astronomy, and Caroline's arrival in England coincided with his mania. He lost interest in training his sister's voice, much to her frustration, and instead suggested she learn to assist him with his astronomical work.

Which she did.

She learned the necessary science and math.

She learned the mechanics of the telescopes William was building so she could properly clean and handle them.

She fed him bits of food when he was too busy to take his hands off said telescope for even a moment.

Caroline was dependent on her parents first, and her brother second. She constantly strove for her independence as her family undermined these efforts, either consciously or subconsciously.

Even if this new life was hard, Caroline was determined to make the best of it. Her positivity shines through her recollections. "When I found that a hand was sometimes wanted when any particular measures were to be made with the lamp micrometer, &c., or a fire to be kept up, or a dish of coffee necessary during a long night's watching, I undertook with pleasure what others might have thought a hardship."[2]

William decided to leave music behind in 1782 when he was offered the position of royal astronomer at Windsor, which came with the salary of £200, half of what he had been making as a musician. This meant that Caroline now had to run their household on half the money she had before.

The move to Windsor also meant that Caroline became William's official assistant, through no choice of her own. Their brother Alex had helped in Bath, but he decided to stay there, so William announced that Caroline would take over his duties.

Caroline was resistant to this at first. She had spent years training her voice and preparing for a musical career. But after a few months of studying with William—and after she became comfortable with the materials—she began to enjoy her new responsibilities:

> In my brother's absence from home, I was of course left solely to amuse myself with my own thoughts, which were anything but cheerful. I found I was to be trained for an

> assistant-astronomer, and by way of encouragement a telescope adapted for "sweeping," consisting of a tube with two glasses, such as are commonly used in a "finder," was given me. I was "to sweep for comets," and I see by my journal that I began August 22nd, 1782, to write down and describe all remarkable appearances I saw in my "sweeps," which were horizontal. But it was not till the last two months of the same year that I felt the least encouragement to spend the star-light nights on a grass-plot covered with dew or hoar frost, without a human being near enough to be within call.[3]

It's also clear that while William might have drafted his sister into service, he respected her talents and invested in them accordingly. In 1783 he built Caroline a new telescope, which she used to "sweep" the heavens.

In July 1786, while William was in Hanover delivering a telescope to the Observatory of Göttingen, Caroline discovered her first comet. She wrote in her recollections, "1 o'clock. —The object of last night *is a comet*."[4] Upon her discovery, Caroline immediately wrote to Charles Blagden, then secretary of the Royal Society, explaining that she had found a new comet, now known as Comet C/1768 P1 (Herschel).

The fact that she discovered the comet when William was away is telling. If Caroline was simply William's loyal assistant with no ambition of her own, why was she sweeping without him? Indeed, all eight of the comets Caroline discovered were found when William was away.

The moment William was elsewhere, Caroline had more time to devote to her own observations, and her discoveries were celebrated by the scientific community near and far. A year later they were honored in a far more significant way when Caroline began to receive an annual pension of £50 from George III for her work as her brother's assistant. This made her the first woman in England to receive an official government position and be paid in an official capacity for her work in astronomy.

By this point, Caroline had discovered five comets.

She was recognized during her own lifetime with a salary, praised and acknowledged by her contemporaries. Those writing about Caroline after her death, however, began to subtly insinuate and question her motives and choices.

In 1788, a year after Caroline began to receive her pension from the government, William married wealthy widow Mary Pitt. With her brother's marriage, Caroline's position in his life changed. She moved out of the main house, where their shared workroom was, and into external lodging. This vital perspective is often treated as a footnote when historians discuss the marriage and Caroline's seeming displeasure with the match.

A year after she finally established herself financially, her brother changed everything. Again.

And she was powerless to stop him.

Caroline stopped writing in her journals the week after William and Mary married. But she recorded her thoughts in various memoranda and letters. It's clear that the early years of the marriage were difficult for Caroline as she adjusted to her new role in her brother's life. She was used to being everything to him, whether she wanted to be or not. Now she had to learn to share.

Which she did. The ever-adaptable Caroline eventually grew to love her new sister-in-law, the evidence clear in her affectionate letters to her, signed off with phrases like, "most obliged and affectionate."[5]

Despite the (perhaps outsize) importance William's marriage has been given, it was not the end of the siblings' partnership, nor did it finish Caroline's work.

In 1798 Caroline sent the Royal Society the Catalogue of Nebulae and Clusters of Stars, a project she undertook after she and William realized that the popular John Flamsteed's catalog wasn't particularly useful for their work, as it was riddled with errors. Caroline's catalog included all of Flamsteed's stars and 560 more that he hadn't included.

William is often credited with the idea for this new catalog, and also the decision to pass it off to Caroline to focus on more exciting astronomical discoveries. But it was this catalog, this painstaking, backbreaking, tedious work, that earned Caroline another formerly unheard-of honor for a woman: In 1835 she and her contemporary Mary Somerville were officially named honorary members of the Royal Astronomical Society, the first and only women admitted for thirty years.

Young, well-bred women of their time weren't told they could be whatever they wanted when they grew up. They were told they could be wives and mothers or, if not that, a burden to their families. The women working in the scientific world of the nineteenth century are products of their time, and to ascribe to them modern ideas about ambition and legacy is to erase an important element they had to constantly fight against.

Caroline's achievements are all the more extraordinary for the circumstances under which they took place. Disfigured and relegated to a life of servitude, Caroline learned not one but several complicated trades as she attempted to build an independent life for herself. In astronomy she found a field in which she could not only help her brother but distinguish herself, which she took pains to do. Caroline made sure each discovery was sent to a suitably impressive colleague and attributed to her.

She left behind as much of her story as she could, and directed her descendants to continue the next chapter. Caroline's niece-in-law, Margaret Brodie Herschel, was fascinated by her brilliant aunt by marriage. It was thanks to Margaret's many questions in letters and during visits that Caroline finally followed through and began to write her autobiography.[6] Margaret's daughters and daughter-in-law continued this legacy, as they ensured Caroline's memoirs were published in 1876 and donated her gold medal from the Royal Astronomical Society to Girton College, which also houses Mary Somerville's papers.

MARY SOMERVILLE

It is deeply unfair but also true that in the nineteenth century, a woman's ability to pursue any kind of academic career, let alone receive recognition for it, was almost entirely dependent on the men in her life. This unfortunate truth is nicely illustrated by the life of the brilliant scientist, mathematician, and thinker Mary Somerville and her two husbands.

Mary Somerville is the kind of woman who deserves many books and much examination from every angle. The scope of her scientific achievements is far beyond this historian's comprehension, and her contemporaries were well aware of her genius. Her obituary in the *Morning Post* declared her the undisputed "Queen of Science."[7]

Mary Fairfax was born into a family with a good name and not a lot of money to go along with it in Scotland in 1780. She was aware of her own intelligence from a young age, and the uphill battle she would have to fight her entire life to receive even a fraction of the same education she would have received if she had simply been born male.

As Mary herself put it, "I was annoyed that my turn for reading was so much disapproved of, and thought it unjust that women should have been given a desire for knowledge if it were wrong to acquire it."[8] It's hard to argue with that logic, but argue the men of Mary's time did.

After a year in a boarding school when she was ten, Mary's formal education ended.

Sources differ on the moment Mary Fairfax showed her true brilliance. Some say she stayed up all night reading her brother's copies of Euclid until her family took her candles away, and that then Mary took this challenge and used it, memorizing the problems and going over them in her head at night, checking to see if she was right in the morning.

Another story goes that Mary was at a tea party when she read a ladies' fashion magazine that featured a mathematical puzzle she became engrossed in solving. She was thwarted until she overheard her painting tutor recommending Euclid's work for better understanding perspective.

In both stories Mary obtains a copy of Euclid with some difficulty and reads it despite her family's disapproval. And either way, it's clear that Mary went out of her way to educate herself.

Mary continued to educate herself even as she married her cousin Captain Samuel Greig, who disapproved of such things, in 1804.

Captain Greig died three short years later, and Mary returned to Scotland with her two small children. Her widowhood allowed her to return to her mathematical studies, and she began a correspondence with several of the leading mathematicians of the time, who, unlike Captain Greig, encouraged her in her pursuit of knowledge.

In 1812 Mary married another cousin, Thomas Somerville. He had a very different opinion about his wife's mathematical career than her first husband and continued to support her studies and work.

The couple moved to London in 1816 and quickly became a part of the leading circles of academics in the city, befriending many familiar names, including William and Caroline Herschel.

Mary published her first paper in 1826 and a year later began work on her first book, a translation of Laplace's *Mécanique Céleste*, which came out in 1831 titled *The Mechanisms of the Heavens*. The book established Mary as an indisputable force to be reckoned with in the mathematical and astronomical world, even if it wasn't a huge commercial success.

Four years after this groundbreaking publication, Mary was admitted as an honorary member, along with Caroline Herschel, to the Royal Astronomical Society. She was also awarded a civil pension to support her work by Prime Minister Sir Robert Peel first and Prime Minister William Lamb subsequently.

All of this was achieved with the support and help of her husband Thomas Somerville, who even acted as editor and note-taker for his wife at times, a reversal of the accepted and expected roles for a husband and wife.

Something history tries to do is isolate exceptional women, but Caroline Herschel and Mary Somerville's friendship, and the extended group they moved within, show us how curious, intellectual women found each other. They also clearly understood the importance of educating the next generation of women scientists. Mary Somerville personally tutored Ada Lovelace, daughter of disreputable poet Byron and Annabella Milbanke, an utterly brilliant scientist in her own right.

Mary's social circle extended beyond just the scientific world. She was also a close personal friend of many of the women discussed throughout this book, including Maria Edgeworth, Mary Berry, and Amelia Opie. These friendships—across academic disciplines, social status, and even geography—remind us that even and especially the most brilliant women in history should be studied in totality.

In the overlap among artists, society ladies, and scientists we can begin to understand what is so fascinating about the Regency. It's a time of incredible change and advancement, with more remarkable women at the foreground than we ever could have imagined.

Of Mary Somerville, her friend Maria Edgeworth wrote, "She has her head in the stars... but her feet firmly on the ground."[9]

JANE MARCET

Jane Haldimand was born in 1769 in London into a wealthy Swiss banking family. Her father, Anthony Francis Haldimand, was a successful merchant and banker who filled his home with intellectual guests. Jane, one of eleven children, took over running the household after her mother, also named Jane, passed away in 1785.

Jane was educated alongside her brothers, receiving an extensive education in languages, botany, and history. She also showed a real talent for art and studied with famed artists Joshua Reynolds and Thomas Lawrence.

In 1799 Jane married a fellow Genevan living in London, Alexander Marcet, a physician trained at the University of Edinburgh. The couple had four children, one of whom, François, went on to become a physicist.

Much like at her father's house, Jane and Alexander created a haven for academics, scientists, artists, and intellectuals in their home. Maria Edgeworth wrote about her visits to the family, painting a picture of a happy, lively, and extremely intellectual household that conducted scientific experiments for fun, like the time she arrived to find the family about to set a "paper fire-balloon" aloft.

Jane was an active participant in the intellectual life of her husband. She attended lectures alongside him whenever possible, including those of noted chemist Humphry Davy. It was after one of these lectures, legend has it, that Jane decided to write an educational text on the ideas she had been presented with, attempting to synthesize the complicated ideas into simpler, more understandable prose.

The initial book, *Conversations on Natural Philosophy*, was written in 1805 but not published until 1819. Instead Jane first published *Conversations on Chemistry* in 1805 anonymously.

The book is written in the form of conversations between a teacher, Mrs. Bryant, and her two pupils, Caroline and Emily. Emily, the older sister, is well behaved, while Caroline is a bit more disruptive, but often furthers the conversation with her inquisitive questions.

Conversations on Chemistry went through sixteen editions in England, and another sixteen in America. In her introduction Jane wrote, "In venturing to offer to the public, and more particularly to the female sex, an introduction to chemistry, the author, herself a woman, conceives that some explanation may be required; and she feels it the more necessary to apologise for the present undertaking, as her knowledge of the subject is but recent, and as she can have no real claims to the title of chemist."[10]

In 1816 Jane published *Conversations on Political Economy*, which summarized and popularized the theories of Adam Smith, Malthus, and David Ricardo. While it was dismissed in some circles as "economics for schoolgirls," this book was responsible for the spread of the principles of classic political economy in fashionable circles in the nineteenth century.

Jane made her subjects accessible. And she revolutionized the idea of widespread scientific education for women. She continued writing for children, especially girls, even as her popularity grew, eschewing more prestigious writing.

In 1820 Jane and Alexander traveled to Geneva with the intent of settling there. Sadly, two years later, Alexander died on a trip back to England. Jane was devastated by his death and suffered a period of depression, one of several throughout her life. She eventually returned to England, where she continued to work and publish.

In 1832 the twelfth edition of *Conversations on Chemistry* was published, and for the first time Jane was named as the author. This caused a bit of a stir in the United States, where the anonymity had allowed a number of (male) authors to take credit for Jane's work. Three years later she published another instant classic, *Mary's Grammar.*

Jane lived the last part of her life with her daughter and her family in London. She died in 1858.

Her legacy can be easily tracked because those she influenced often wrote about it. Famous chemist and physicist Michael Faraday credited Jane's *Conversations on Chemistry* as introducing him to the topic. Harriet Martineau, the popular Victorian social historian, also cited Jane as an influence.

Mary Somerville herself said, "No one at this time can duly estimate the importance of Mrs Marcet's scientific works."[11]

MARY ANNING

Have you ever heard the saying "She sells seashells by the seashore"? It's a popular tongue-twister that originated at the end of the nineteenth century, and since the middle of the twentieth century has been inextricably linked to Mary Anning.

There's no direct or even circumstantial evidence that Mary Anning inspired the tongue-twister, but the association persists. Mary Anning did not sell seashells by the seashore. In actuality she had a shop in the seaside resort town of Lyme Regis, where she sold fossils that she found along the Blue Lias cliffs.

Mary entered the world of paleontology at a moment of immense discoveries and intense speculation and fear over what they meant. The predominantly devoutly Christian scientific community was coming face-to-face with incontrovertible proof of evolution.

Mary's father, Richard, died in 1810, leaving the family struggling financially. She spent the rest of her life working to provide for them. Despite her talent for finding fossils, Mary never received the kind of financial compensation that would have lifted her family out of poverty.

In 1811 Mary and her brother Joseph were fossil hunting when they spotted a dark, glistening *something* among the cliffs of Lyme Regis. Mary spent weeks excavating the entire skeleton, with the help of local laborers and sometimes her brother and mother.

Eventually the discovery was officially named an ichthyosaurus, a name created by putting the Greek words for "fish" and "lizard" together. It was bought for £23 by local landowner Henry Hoste Henley, who turned around and sold the specimen to Bullock's Museum of Natural Curiosities, which in turn sold it to the British Museum for £48.

In 1823 Mary was the undisputed discoverer of a plesiosaurus, a discovery so shocking that Georges Cuvier, the famous French zoologist, called it a fake.

A friend of Mary's, William Conybeare, had discovered the first head of such a skeleton and came up with the name, meaning "near to reptile." Mary immediately sent a drawing of her discovery to Conybeare, who could hardly believe what he was looking at, but knew that they were onto something.

In France, Georges Cuvier thought differently. He examined Mary's drawing and believed the neck to be impossibly long. He wrote to Conybeare throwing doubt on Mary's discovery and putting her reputation at serious risk.

A debate was called at the Royal Geological Society, to which Mary was not invited. Conybeare defended Mary's find and Cuvier was finally forced to admit that he, not Mary, had been wrong.

Mary sold her plesiosaurus to the Duke of Buckingham, who paid £110—the most anyone had paid for a single specimen up to that point.

In our collective imagination, Mary is a little old lady, bent over with age as she sells simple seashells. But Mary actually died of cancer at forty-seven and never reached old age.

This popular image is a mix of the old tongue-twister along with one of the only images of Mary drawn in her lifetime, a sketch of her working by Henry Thomas De la Beche, which shows Mary as a stooped old lady, wrapped in a large cloak, pickax in hand.

De la Beche meant no disrespect. A friend of Mary's from childhood, Henry spent a considerable amount of time and energy making sure that Mary received at least some financial compensation for her contributions to science. As well as the sketch of Mary working, he drew the famous print *Duria Antiquior—A More Ancient Dorset*, based on the fossils Mary had found. [Figure 12] Then he arranged for her to receive some of the proceeds from sales of the print.

Thomas was not Mary's only protector/defender. He collaborated with fellow scientist William Conybeare on a paper based on Mary's findings, and the pair helped defend her against Georges Cuvier's charges of fakery. Lieutenant Colonel Thomas Birch, another noted fossil collector, also took an interest in Mary and her mother, Molly. After learning of their financial struggles, Birch decided to sell his collection of fossils—largely collected by the Annings—in a noted auction that raised over £400.

Mary was also friends with noted local paleontology enthusiast the Reverend William Buckland. The pair spent many years hunting for fossils together, and the trips were important enough that Buckland's daughter mentioned them in her biography of her father: "The vacations of his earliest Oxford time were spent near Lyme Regis. For years afterwards local gossip preserved traditions of his adventures with that geological celebrity Mary Anning, in whose company he was to be seen wading up to his knees in search of fossils in the Blue Lias."[12]

Mary's friendships with men were the subject of some speculation during and after her lifetime. People questioned the motives behind the generous help provided by Birch and De la Beche, but there is no evidence of anything other than friendship and mutual respect. And Mary didn't just enjoy strong friendships with brilliant men; she had many close female friends as well. The Philpot sisters, especially Elizabeth, were Mary's constant companions.

SPOTLIGHT ON THE PHILPOT SISTERS

The Philpot sisters are a perfect example of the tantalizing clues the historical record has left us of other women active in the sciences in the nineteenth century. Elizabeth (1780–1857), Mary (1777–1838), and Margaret (d. 1845) Philpot arrived in Lyme Regis in 1805. They moved into Morley Cottage on Silver Street, a house rented for them by their solicitor brother John.

The three sisters lived together and assembled an impressive collection of fossils. A neighbor, Selina Hallett, described it like this: "Several cases with glass tops and shallow drawers all down the front stood in the dining room and the back parlor and upstairs on the landing, all full of fossils with a little ticket on each of them."[13]

Some twenty years older than Mary Anning, Elizabeth took her under her wing. The two formed a close friendship, writing to each other about their discoveries and sharing news of each other in letters to other friends.

The Philpots were at the center of Lyme Regis's active community of amateur scientists. They regularly entertained visitors at Morley Cottage such as the eccentric William Buckland, the first professor of geology at Oxford and husband to Mary Buckland, another woman working in the field.

Details about the Philpots are tantalizingly few and far between. They appear in Mary Anning's letters, as well as many of their scientific contemporaries. Some of Elizabeth's letters to Mary survive, along with her impressive fossil collection: Over four hundred specimens are now housed at the Oxford Museum of Natural History, just waiting for an intrepid historian to discover them and give them the attention they deserve.

(BACK TO MARY ANNING)

In 1824 Mary also befriended a new arrival to Lyme Regis, a young invalid woman named Frances Augusta Bell. When Frances returned to London a few months later, she and Mary struck up a correspondence. The letters reveal a depth of feeling between the women that has led some historians and artists to question Mary's sexual orientation. This speculation has led to a movie, *Ammonite*, written and directed by Francis Lee, starring Kate Winslet as Mary Anning and Saoirse Ronan as Charlotte Murchison, another woman in the extended network of women in the nineteenth-century scientific world.

Perhaps the best distillation of her contemporaries' opinions can be seen in Lady Harriet Silvester's thoughts after visiting Mary Anning:

> The extraordinary thing in this young woman is that she has made herself so thoroughly acquainted with the science that the moment she finds any bones she knows to what tribe they belong. She fixes the bones on a frame with cement and then makes drawings and has them engraved... It is certainly a wonderful instance of divine favour—that this poor, ignorant girl should be so blessed, for by reading and application she has arrived to that degree of knowledge as to be in the habit of writing and talking with professors and other clever men on the subject, and they all acknowledge that she understands more of the science than anyone else in this kingdom.[14]

Despite all the acclaim and admiration she received, Mary still had to deal with the most inconvenient truth of her birth—her gender. The scientific world of the Regency simply wasn't ready for all she had to offer, but that didn't stop her and her female friends from fighting for their space.

MARY BUCKLAND

Mary Buckland, née Morland, was born in 1797 to Benjamin Morland, a solicitor, and his wife, Harriet, who died soon after Mary's birth.

Mary was raised by her father and his new wife and half siblings. She was a thoughtful and curious child who evinced an interest in the natural sciences from a young age. She was encouraged in this by her father, who arranged for her to study with Sir Christopher Pegge, a professor of anatomy at Oxford. Pegge was fond enough of Mary to leave her "his mineral cabinets and all the minerals and fossils contained in them at the time of my decease and all my books of natural history and comparative anatomy as a mark of my esteem and regard for her."[15]

Through her studies with Pegge, Mary learned to become a skilled scientific illustrator. Her services were much in demand by leading scientists like Georges Cuvier and William Conybeare.

Indeed, the story of Mary meeting her eventual husband, William Buckland, shows that her fame preceded her. The pair were traveling to Dorsetshire and both happened to be reading the same new text from Georges Cuvier and began talking about it. It is then that William remarked that the woman he was talking to must be Miss Morland, the very woman he was traveling to deliver a letter of recommendation to.

The couple were married in 1825, and took a yearlong honeymoon touring geological sites across Europe. They had nine children, five of whom lived to adulthood. Their son Frank Buckland became an important zoologist while one of their daughters, Mary Oke Buckland Gordon, became an author. She wrote a biography of her famous father.

Mary raised and educated her children around the work she and her husband were doing. [Figure 13] Her son Frank later wrote, "Not only was she a pious, amiable, and excellent helpmate to my father; but being naturally endowed with great mental powers, habits of perseverance and order, tempered by excellent judgement, she materially assisted her husband in his literary labours, and often gave to them a polish which added not a little to their merit..."[16]

Mary's husband was a famous and celebrated scientist. He published several important works including *Reliquiae Diluvianae* (1823) and *Geology and Mineralogy* (1836), both of which were greatly enhanced by Mary's illustrations. Despite all the work Mary did for him, William was still disapproving of women in the sciences. In 1831 the British Association for the Advancement of Science was formed and Buckland named president. The association debated allowing women to join, but Buckland wrote to Roderick Murchison: "Everyone agrees that, if the meeting is to be of scientific utility, ladies ought not to attend the reading of the papers and especially at Oxford as it would at once turn the thing into a sort of Albermarle-dilettante-meeting, instead of a serious philosophical union of working men."[17]

This attitude is particularly frustrating in the face of how much Mary did for her husband. She supported him wholeheartedly in his career, traipsing all over the country and the world in search of fossils, often while pregnant or caring for small children. She reconstructed fossils for his study and illustrated many more fossils, countless of which ended up in Buckland's published work. Many of the fossils she reconstructed for her husband's eventual use are now in the collection of the Oxford University Museum of Natural History.

In 1845 William Buckland was named dean of Westminster and the family relocated. Mary turned her attentions to educating the local children, teaching geography at the village school. However, William's physical and mental health had begun to deteriorate in 1842, and he passed away in 1856.

Mary spent the last years of her life continuing to promote her husband's work and do her own experiments, often with the help of her daughter. She died in 1857.

CONCLUSION

In 1832 Charles Lyell, a professor of geology at Oxford, prepared to give a series of lectures based on his new book *Principles of Geology*. All university lectures were closed to women, and Lyell planned to follow tradition despite the fact that he was assisted and helped immeasurably in his work by his fiancée, Mary Elizabeth Horner. Lyell only relented when Roderick Murchison refused to attend the lectures unless his wife and fellow geologist Charlotte Murchison could as well.

This was a major, if short-lived, victory for women studying paleontology in the nineteenth century. After two lectures, women were once again banned. But Lyell's mind at least seemed to have been changed. He resigned from the Oxford faculty and continued his lecture series at the Royal Institution, where women were allowed to attend.

The scientific world of the nineteenth century was small, and this episode highlights that. It also underscores the difficulties women in the sciences faced, even from the men they lived with and worked beside. These women had to fight for recognition in public and private.

In 2010, to celebrate the Royal Society's 350th anniversary, a committee was convened to pick the ten British women who had had the most influence on science. Mary Anning, Caroline Herschel, and Mary Somerville were all included—underscoring the importance of Regency women to the history of science.

It is a truth universally acknowledged that one brilliant woman in history indicates a previously unstudied network of other brilliant women. The women working in the scientific world of the nineteenth century are certainly proof positive of this. While they might have relied on their husbands, brothers, or fathers for financial support and social security, it was their fellow female scientists who understood their unique challenges and the sweetness of their victories.

Recommended Reading

Arianrhod, Robyn. *Émilie Du Châtelet, Mary Somerville and the Newtonian Revolution*. Oxford University Press, 2012.

Brück, Mary. *Women in Early British and Irish Astronomy: Stars and Satellites*. Springer, 2009.

Creese, Mary. *Ladies in the Laboratory? American and British Women in Science, 1800–1900: A Survey of Their Contributions to Research*. Scarecrow Press, 1998.

Dare, Tessa. *A Week to Be Wicked*. Avon, 2012.

Elliott, Cara. *To Sin with a Scoundrel*. Forever, 2010.

Emling, Shelley. *The Fossil Hunter: Dinosaurs, Evolution, and the Woman Whose Discoveries Changed the World*. Macmillan, 2009.

Holmes, Richard. *The Age of Wonder: How the Romantic Generation Discovered the Beauty and Terror of Science*. HarperCollins, 2008.

Hoskin, Michael. *Caroline Herschel's Autobiographies*. Science History Publications, 2003.

Hoskin, Michael. *Caroline Herschel: Priestess of the New Heavens*. Science History Publications, 2013.

Kölbl-Ebert, Martina. "Sketching Rocks and Landscape: Drawing as a Female Accomplishment in the Service of Geology." *Earth Sciences History* 31, no. 2 (2012): 270–86.

Milan, Courtney. *Talk Sweetly to Me*. 2014.

Pascoe, Judith. *The Hummingbird Cabinet: A Rare and Curious History of Romantic Collecting*. Cornell University Press, 2006.

Patterson, Elizabeth C. "Mary Somerville." *British Journal of the History of Science* 4, no. 4 (1969).

[Figure 12] Thomas De la Beche. *Duria Antiquior.* 1830. *(Ichthyosaurus/Natural History Museum, London, UK/Bridgeman Images.)*

[Figure 13] August Edouart. *William Buckland and his wife Mary and son Frank, Examining Buckland's Natural History Collection.* Circa 1828.

CHAPTER SIX

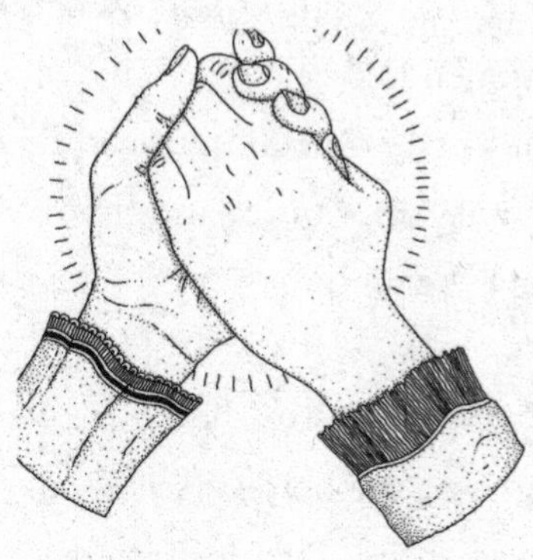

The Fairer Sex

At Shibden Hall she had them all
The fairer sex fell under her spell
Dapper and bright
She held them tight
Handsome Anne seduced them well
Gentleman Jack
Oh Gentleman Jack
Watch your back you're under attack

—O'Hooley and Tidow, opening song for
HBO's *Gentleman Jack*, produced in 2012

Gentleman Jack was the real-life nickname of Anne Lister, one of the most famous queer people of the nineteenth century during and after her life. Out and even married to a woman, Anne ruled her corner of Halifax as a wealthy landowner after she inherited her uncle's estate Shibden Hall.

In 2017 HBO and BBC One announced that they were developing a TV show about Anne Lister and her exploits, based on the coded diaries she kept throughout her life. The series premiered in 2019.

Gentleman Jack follows Anne as she meets, seduces, and eventually marries her neighbor, the heiress Ann Walker.

Gentleman Jack was an immediate success, and a second season was ordered almost immediately after the premiere episode.

Modern audiences were hungry for representation of the queer people we know existed during the Regency. This representation has appeared in the world of fiction through pioneering works of historical fiction like Emma Donoghue's *Life Mask* based on the real life of Anne Damer, sculptor and rumored lesbian, and her love affair with the celebrated actress Eliza Farren, who went on to marry the twelfth Earl of Derby.

Romance novels have also filled the void, with queer characters taking center stage and getting their happy endings in works by authors like Cat Sebastian, KJ Charles, EE Ottoman, and Lily Maxton. In June 2019 Avon Books released their first historical lesbian title, *The Lady's Guide to Celestial Mechanics* by Olivia Waite, which features a heroine studying astronomy much like Caroline Herschel.

The question of identification, self and otherwise, when discussing sexuality historically is a difficult one to be sure, but it shouldn't stand in the way of considering the queer women of the Regency together and separately.

Some of the women in this chapter left behind written proof of their love for other women. Others remain tantalizingly silent on the subject.

Absence of proof is not itself proof of anything.

The four women profiled in this chapter offer different versions of queer identity in the Regency. While there are shared themes and through-lines in their stories, each one is unique. They remind us that queer identity has never been a monolith.

They also show us that queer people were able to carve out happy and fulfilling lives in nineteenth-century England. Despite sometimes critical and satirizing press, the women in this chapter sought out people who would love and accept them as they were. In doing so, they gave us a historical record that shows there were always people who believe love is love is love.

ANNE DAMER

As the only female sculptor to exhibit at the Royal Academy in the nineteenth century, Anne Seymour Damer was a famous character in her own time. She was also the subject of persistent rumors surrounding the close relationships she enjoyed with women. Unlike other queer figures in the Regency, Anne never took any public action to confirm or deny the rumors. She simply lived her life.

Anne is a bundle of contradictions. In some ways she followed expectations, as with her (unhappy but socially advantageous) marriage. In other ways she confounded her contemporaries, for example by refusing to stay on the traditional path following her husband's death. Anne is a fascinating example of an aristocratic Regency woman who practiced her art for love and money, facing down public mockery with the support of her friends.

Anne Seymour Damer, née Conway, was born on November 8, 1748, into a world of immense wealth and privilege. Her parents, Henry Seymour Conway, an army officer and politician, and Caroline Bruce, Lady Ailesbury, knew everybody who was anybody in late-eighteenth-century British society. Their marriage was a love match, and Caroline's second marriage after the death of her much older husband, the Earl of Ailesbury. The couple were popular hosts at their London townhouse in Soho Square and at their country seat, Park Place.

Anne was the couple's only child (Lady Ailesbury had a daughter from her first marriage). She was doted on and given every advantage by her parents, and by all accounts was a charming and intelligent child. But the Conways were in high demand as emissaries for England, they were frequently abroad, and in the time-honored tradition of all children left behind, Anne received a series of exotic and unusual gifts, including a pet monkey.

When they traveled, the Conways had the perfect guardian for their precocious daughter—their dear friend Horace Walpole.

SPOTLIGHT ON HORACE WALPOLE

Horace Walpole was one of the most colorful, and important, characters of the early-nineteenth-century world. Wealthy, connected, a terrible gossip, and a celebrated author, Walpole—much like his protégée Anne Damer—lived life on his own terms.

Born in 1717 to Robert Walpole, the prime minister of England, and his wife, Catherine, Horace was destined for greatness. He wrote the celebrated Gothic novel *The Castle of Otranto* in 1764. In 1791 he ascended to the peerage as he inherited the title of Earl of Orford.

Despite this impressive lineage, and the attendant pressures to produce an heir, Horace remained unmarried his whole life. He enjoyed extremely close friendships with a number of men, including Anne's father, Henry Conway, as well as women. Much like Anne, Horace faced rumors surrounding his sexuality his entire life. Also like Anne, he ignored them and continued on just as he pleased.

Horace's great love was his estate Strawberry Hill, which he turned into a Gothic masterpiece. There he established his own printing press, where he printed his friends' works.

Horace lived a fascinating life. And he narrated the whole thing through the endless letters he wrote to friends and contemporaries. He left his correspondence to the Berry sisters, and his beloved Strawberry Hill to Anne.

Walpole's letters read like a Rolodex of the wealthy and powerful of late-eighteenth-century England. As son of the first prime minister, Walpole enjoyed a unique position fusing his roles as an arbiter of taste, highly connected political figure, and patron of the arts into something wholly him.

(BACK TO ANNE DAMER)

Walpole had a reputation for collecting talented young women, and Anne was no exception. He extolled her virtues in the many letters he sent around the world, and encouraged her in her artistic pursuits. It was not needlework or the expected watercolors or evening oil portraits that Anne was interested in creating.

Along with the de rigueur French and Italian, Anne also mastered Latin and Greek. From a very early age she evinced an admiration for the classical world and style. She wanted to join the pantheon of classical artists she most admired: the sculptors.

In all things, Anne was an original. But her career choice—the choice to join the almost exclusively male domain of sculpting—was so unusual that it swiftly created a mythology surrounding her decision.

The story goes that she was walking with her father's secretary, the soon-to-be-famous historian David Hume, when they ran into a boy in the street carrying a tray with several plaster figures on it. After Anne dismissed the boy's artistic attempts, Hume asserted that no matter Anne's many talents, she couldn't produce anything like the boy had. The legend goes that Anne was so determined to prove Hume wrong that she devoted her life to becoming a sculptor.

Before she could do that, however, even the inimitable Anne had to follow the expected life path of an aristocratic young lady and get married.

There were many candidates for her hand, including at least two dukes. But in 1767 Anne married John Damer, the eldest son of Lord Milton. He was also a rake and a gambling addict. Walpole had his misgivings about the marriage, but he was still intimately involved in the negotiations. His letters indicate that while he knew about Damer's past, he also knew Anne's parents were thrilled with the match and he wanted to support them. Society deemed it a good pairing. Anne's feelings are not recorded, and may not have mattered. The powers that be had spoken, and Anne and John were married.

The truth, of course, was much more complicated. Anne and John were estranged within a year, and spent the rest of their nine-year marriage apart. In the face of this failure, Anne often retreated to Strawberry Hill and the circle of friends surrounding Horace Walpole. There she met the leading thinkers, artists, politicians, and academics of the day.

Seeking refuge from her unhappy marriage, in the early 1770s Anne became fast friends with two of the leading society ladies of her day: Georgiana, Duchess of Devonshire, and Lady Melbourne.

SPOTLIGHT ON GEORGIANA, DUCHESS OF DEVONSHIRE

Georgiana is one of those one-name people, like Madonna or Rihanna.

Born in 1757 to John Spencer, later Earl Spencer, and his wife Georgiana, Georgiana the younger enjoyed an idyllic childhood.

That ended with her marriage at seventeen to William Cavendish, the fifth Duke of Devonshire. The marriage was a deeply unhappy one.

As the Duchess of Devonshire, Georgiana was one of the most important social and political hostesses of her day. She threw herself into her duties, and emerged as an arbiter of fashion, to put it mildly. Everything she did and wore was watched, commented on, and often copied by her peers. She used this to support a number of female artists through noted patronage.

Despite her beauty and social success, the Duke of Devonshire had little interest in his young wife. Instead he carried on a passionate affair with Lady Elizabeth Foster, a close friend of Georgiana's. Rather than fight the situation, Georgiana allowed Lady Elizabeth to live with them, creating one of the most unusual domestic arrangements of the time. This love triangle explains why Georgiana looked outside her marriage for companionship, forming close attachments to a number of female friends and notoriously taking several famous lovers.

Georgiana is often remembered for the intersection of her scandalous personal life and her role as a leader in society and politics. She blended the two by carrying on an affair with Charles Grey, who served as prime minister of the United Kingdom from 1830 to 1834.

While Georgiana and the duke's marriage was notoriously unhappy, it still produced three daughters who carried on Georgiana's legacy after her death in 1806. She was so famous that upon her death the Prince of Wales was said to remark, "The best natured and the best bred woman in England is gone."

(BACK TO ANNE DAMER)

Ever dramatic, Anne immortalized her new friendship with Georgiana and Lady Melbourne in a painting she commissioned from Daniel Gardner in 1775. The women are shown as the three witches from *Macbeth*, surrounding a cauldron. [Figure 14]

As famous, rich, and celebrated as these women were, each had her own set of personal and public struggles. It's fascinating to see them banding together as a friend group to face these difficulties. We often think of historical women, especially brilliant ones, as isolated. Anne and her friends chose to be remembered exactly as that: friends.

Their choice to be portrayed as Macbeth's witches is certainly provocative! Enough that their contemporary Lady Mary Coke wrote about the decision in her diary: "I daresay they think their charms more irresistible than all the magick of the Witches."[1]

Framing the women as witches shows a keen awareness of the gossip surrounding them, their friendship, and their political machinations. All three were devoted members of the Whig party who campaigned vigorously for their preferred candidate Charles Fox in 1784 to much public scorn. This included an array of caricatures poking fun at everything from the fashionable clothing the women wore to campaign, to more serious charges of exchanging sexual favors for votes. Instead of apologizing for their political meddling, the women chose one of the most iconic images of women meddling in the fates of men as their representation.

There are two versions of the portrait, and their differences illuminate a certain truth of history. In the first Georgiana wears a tiara, denoting her higher social status. The portrait is laden with symbolism. Cats climb on Lady Melbourne, while Anne's dress is decorated with scales of justice, skull and bones, and animals. It's a careful show of strength, humor, and awareness for a public audience.

The second portrait is far less formal. The three women hold hands, and all wear the same traditional black witch's hat. Lady Melbourne probably commissioned the second version, as it hung at her daughter's country estate Panshanger. It is a much more personal record of the friendship the women shared, highlighting a certain version of history, the one the women have chosen for themselves.

As Macbeth's witches, Anne and her friends flipped the script, becoming the ones with the real power, scheming behind the scenes to achieve their desired ends. Of course, this fantasy only lasted so long. While Anne busied herself with her friends and family, her unhappy marriage continued to deteriorate. In 1776 her husband killed himself after a night of bad luck at the gambling tables.

Anne was suddenly a widow. And she had an enormous amount of debt to pay off. Her husband had racked up over £70,000 in gambling debt. Lord Milton was no help; distraught and furious at his son's death, he blamed Anne and demanded she pay the debts herself.

In the face of tragedy and hardship, Anne showed her true strength of character. She sold her jewels and went to live with her half sister, trying to save money anywhere she could.

After paying back the debts, Anne was left to consider a very different life than she had been living, financially at least. She spent some time traveling with her aunt, to Spain, Portugal, Italy, and France. Finally she settled back in London, setting up a studio and turning back to her childhood dream of becoming a sculptor.

Walpole wrote to a friend that he had never seen Anne so happy. But amid this journey to find herself, for the first time Anne also faced public rumors about her extremely close and passionate friendships with women.

In 1777 a couplet poem written by William Coombe appeared: *The First of April; Or, The Triumphs of Folly.* It was not the last, or the most explicit, but it was the first public accusation of indifference at her husband's death, and of finding comfort with her fellow widows.

The twin truths of Anne's life seem inextricably linked: her pursuit of a traditionally male career and her passionate female friendships, which she refused to displace with a second marriage.

As her fame as a sculptor grew, the rumors continued. In 1789 the two were connected forever in the historical record with the appearance of a satirical print titled *The Damerian Apollo.* [Figure 15] In the image, Anne is at work. She is seated, with her mallet raised above her head. Her chisel penetrates the buttocks of the statue of Apollo in front of her. Apollo gestures toward another statue in front of him, in which a man and woman embrace. They stand on a pedestal that says STUDIES FROM NATURE.

The meaning is clear. There is a natural order to things, a natural way of relationships. Man and woman go together.

The Damerian Apollo was put on display at William Holland's exhibition room in Oxford Street for all to come and see. This was a public and embarrassing calling-out.

We don't have an existing record of Anne's reaction to this particular offensive print. But we do have letters between Anne and her friend Edward Jerningham showing that Anne was aware of rumors being printed in the press, asking Jerningham to keep an eye out, and finally telling him she doesn't wish him to speak to an editor about printing the rumors. It is particularly striking to see Anne refuse the help of her friends in combating these stories.

Anne refused to go the "natural" way. She held stubbornly to her independence, turning down multiple marriage proposals. Free of one unhappy marriage, she was loath to enter another.

Seventeen eighty-nine was also the year that Horace Walpole introduced Anne to Mary Berry, another one of his protégées and the woman with whom Anne would spend the rest of her life in an emotionally passionate relationship.[2]

Mary Berry and her sister Agnes had met Walpole a year earlier, and quickly charmed him. Much as with Anne, Walpole encouraged the sisters in their writing and art, and let them live in Little Strawberry Hill, a house on his estate.

Anne and Mary became fast friends. But this friendship was different, both publicly and privately, than her past dalliances.

Anne and Mary have sometimes been considered in the tradition of "romantic friendship" or a Boston marriage. The term refers to the cohabitation of two women, and has traditionally referred to a chaste relationship. It's usually associated with Henry James's novel *The Bostonians* (1886), which tells the story of two women living together and struggling with their feelings for one another.

It is hard not to editorialize here. The passion in Anne and Mary's letters is clear. They were each other's confidantes and confessors. They helped each other through heartache and family drama. They were partners in art, working together on Mary's play *Fashionable Friends*. Contemporaries remarked on their devotion to one another. Adhering to the sentimental tradition of the day, Anne gave Mary a portrait of herself by Richard Cosway. Cosway also captured Anne and Mary in an unguarded moment at Strawberry Hill, the sketch of which jumps out at a modern viewer for the connection between the two women, despite their lack of physical closeness in the image. [Figure 16] Instead Anne and Mary are shown sitting across a table from one another, the affection between them clear on their respective faces.

Anne and Mary's mutual friend, the playwright Joanna Baillie, wrote extensively to both women. Amid all the gossip and comments on Mary's latest play, there is a clear pattern. In every letter, Joanna asks after Anne or Mary. The two women are inextricably linked in her mind. They are a pair, a partnership.

After Walpole's death in 1797, the women lived together at Strawberry Hill. They devoted themselves to honoring Walpole's memory by giving tours of the house to curious visitors, and they amused themselves and their friends by putting up amateur theatricals in the theater.

They also traveled together, which was actually more socially acceptable than either of them traveling alone. In 1802 they went to Paris, where they were granted an audience with Napoleon as well as his wife, Josephine, and Napoleon's mother. This paved the way for a later visit during the Hundred Days in 1815 when Anne presented Napoleon with a marble bust of Charles Fox and he gave her a bejeweled snuffbox.

Anne's career continued to flourish. Between 1784 and 1818 she exhibited thirty-two works as an honorary exhibitor at the Royal Academy. She traveled to Italy frequently and studied with masters there, ever on a quest to perfect her art.

Anne died in 1828. She was buried with the ashes of her dog and her sculptor's tools. She left behind hundreds of works of art, letters, journals, and even a novel, but no conclusive record of her feelings toward friends like Mary Berry, Lady Melbourne, and Eliza Farren.

It is impossible to definitively identify Anne Damer as a lesbian, at least with the currently available sources. But the fact that she was identified as such during her lifetime, even if it was maliciously intended, means that she is an intrinsic part of the conversation on queer identity in Regency England.

It is undeniable that Anne thrived, despite the rumors surrounding her sexuality. She enjoyed a wide circle of friends and received critical accolades for her art. She also refused to adhere to the societal norms of the day, in more ways than one. She left behind a legacy of perseverance in staying true to one's own self.

ANNE LISTER

In some ways, Anne Lister is worlds away from Anne Damer. With Damer, all we can do is read between the lines, search for clues, and make our conclusions.

Anne Lister is a nineteenth-century historian's dream. It can be terribly frustrating to have theories and hunches but no way to verify them. Anne solved this problem by leaving behind journals documenting the quotidian of her daily and emotional life from the age of sixteen. The fact that many of these thoughts were those of lust and love for other women makes the journal all the more fascinating and important.

Aware of the explosive nature of what she was writing, Anne wrote the journals in a code she called crypthand, a mix of algebra and the Greek alphabet. The first journals are just a few sheets of loose-leaf paper, but as Anne began to take her journaling more seriously she started to use school exercise books and finally hard-backed notebooks. There are sixty-six hundred pages of material and over four million words.

While Anne was clearly aware of the transgressive nature of her sexuality, she did nothing to hide her truth. In fact she dressed all in black, frequently in men's clothing, and she earned the nickname Gentleman Jack from the local Halifax community, indicating that there was something distinctly masculine about Anne's appearance and presentation. She lived openly with and went through church marriage rituals with a woman, her neighbor Ann Walker—a courtship and marriage chronicled in the aforementioned television show *Gentleman Jack*.

Anne was as openly queer as one could possibly be in Regency England. She's usually discussed as an anomaly. But what is clear from Anne's journals is that there were any number of ready and willing female partners just within her local community in Halifax, and even more when she traveled abroad.

Born on April 3, 1791, to Jeremy Lister, a captain in the American War for Independence, and Rebecca Battle, Anne was one of six children. Three of her brothers died in infancy, while her brother Samuel died in 1813 in a boating accident. She had a younger sister, Marian.

The death of her brother meant that Anne would inherit Shibden Hall, her uncle James's estate. She moved there in 1815 with her sister, happy to escape her parents' house.

Anne's aunt and uncle were much more permissive than her parents, and Anne quickly gained a reputation in Halifax for her masculine behavior and appearance.

Unlike Anne Damer or the Ladies of Llangollen, there is no doubt that Anne Lister unequivocally identified as a lover of women and enjoyed physical relationships with a number of them. In 1821 Anne wrote, "I love and only love the fairer sex and thus beloved by them in turn, my heart revolts from any love but theirs."[3] She referred to this preference as her "oddity."

Anne was a wealthy and independent woman, and she lived as such. She was the first woman to be elected to the committee of the Halifax branch of the Literary and Philosophical Society. On her land she developed coal mining, from which future generations would benefit. (This change in industry was a focus of *Gentleman Jack*, positioning Anne as particularly progressive and industrious in her mining attempts.) She traveled, and was the first woman to ascend Mount Perdu in the Pyrenees. In 1838 she became the first person to ascend Mount Vignemale.

Even with such an adventurous nature, Anne craved a respectable relationship. In 1823 she wrote in her journal, "But I mean to amend at five & thirty & retire with credit. I shall have a good fling before then. Four years. And in the meantime I shall make my avenae communes, my wild oats common. I shall domiciliate then."[4]

And a "good fling" she had. Before she settled down, Anne enjoyed a number of tumultuous and passionate relationships both local and international. The great love of her life was Mariana Lawton. They were introduced by another of Anne's lovers, Isabella Norcliffe. Isabella desperately wanted to settle down with Anne, but Anne did not approve of her drinking, and she rejected Isabella in favor of her friend Mariana. Isabella never got over Anne's rejection and remained single her whole life.

Mariana, on the other hand, married Charles Lawton soon after meeting Anne and starting a relationship with her. Anne never fully got over this betrayal, but the pair also continued their relationship long after the marriage, and their correspondence even longer than that.

After years of affairs, Anne settled down in 1834 with a neighboring heiress, Ann Walker.

Ann was an interesting choice for many reasons. Unlike the passionate and turbulent love affairs of her youth, Anne's relationship with Ann was much more domestic and traditional. Ann was known as a quiet, gently bred young woman. Choosing Ann shows just how much Anne cared about being socially accepted and living as respectable a life as possible. Their union made sense in financial and geographic terms. The two went through various marriage rituals and formally joined their business interests, writing each other into their respective wills.

In 1840 they traveled through Belgium, Holland, Denmark, Sweden, and Finland to reach Russia. There Anne caught a fever

Timeline of Anne's Lovers

1806
Eliza Raine

Fellow pupil at the Manor School in York
The relationship ended due to Eliza's mental health

1810
Isabella Norcliffe

Alias: Tib
Became friends, and were occasional lovers for the rest of Anne's life
Isabella introduced Anne to Mariana Lawton, whom Anne left her for
Isabella stayed single her whole life

and died at the base of the Caucasus Mountains. Ann brought her body back to Halifax, where she was buried in the parish church.

SARAH PONSONBY AND ELEANOR BUTLER: THE LADIES OF LLANGOLLEN

Unlike Anne Damer and Anne Lister and their various partners, the Ladies of Llangollen cannot be considered separately. The two are tied together by a single, life-changing choice. Sarah Ponsonby and Eleanor Butler, known collectively as the Ladies of Llangollen,

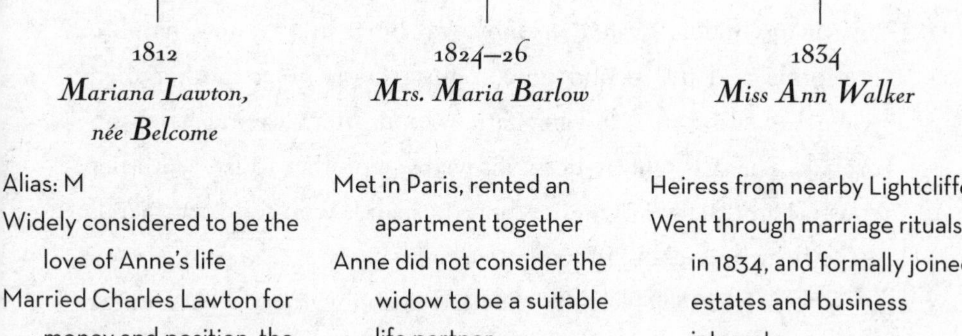

eloped in 1778 and lived together for the rest of their lives, becoming figures of great interest to their contemporaries.

Despite their unconventional living arrangement, the Ladies maintained that their relationship was chaste. They exist on a spectrum somewhere between Anne Damer and Anne Lister, and provide a third example of queer identity in Regency England.

Eleanor Charlotte Butler was born in Cambrai, France, in 1739 to prominent Irishman Walter Butler and Eleanor de Montmorency Morres. Eleanor was the third daughter and quickly followed by a brother, John, born a year later. She spent most of her childhood in France, educated at the English Benedictine House in Cambrai.

She returned to Kilkenny in 1768, to see her brother convert to Anglicanism and marry Lady Anne Wandesford. Her sisters had already married, leaving Eleanor as the sole single Butler sibling.

Meanwhile...Sarah Ponsonby was born in 1755 to Chambre Ponsonby and his second wife, Louisa Lyons. Her mother died when she was three and her father soon after, leaving Sarah an orphan. She was sent by her widowed stepmother to live with her cousin Lady Betty Fownes and her husband, who soon sent Sarah off to boarding school in Kilkenny.

Where thirteen-year-old Sarah Ponsonby met twenty-nine-year-old Eleanor Butler.

We don't know how they met, or much at all about their early interactions. And while that age gap might raise modern eyebrows, it was seemingly uninteresting enough for none of their contemporaries to comment on it.

Their biographer Elizabeth Mavor (who insists the Ladies'

relationship was emotionally intense but physically chaste) notes the similarity between the Ladies' later plans and a 1762 account by Sarah Scott of philanthropic female retirement, *A Description of Millenium Hall*. But we have no proof the Ladies knew about Scott's work. We have no idea where they found inspiration for their unprecedented choice to abandon their expected futures for the complete unknown, together.

What we do know is that in 1773, Sarah Ponsonby left school to live with her cousin Lady Fownes and her husband, Sir William, and soon after began writing to family friends that Sir William had made inappropriate sexual advances toward her and seemed to have designs on marrying her after his wife's anticipated death.

Meanwhile, Eleanor's relationship with her mother had deteriorated as she discovered her mother's plans to send her to a convent.

Eleanor and Sarah shared secret letters detailing their unhappy future prospects and began forming a plan to run away together and set up a house away from their families.

On March 30, 1778, the pair escaped from their respective homes wearing men's clothing and carrying pistols. They met up and traveled to Waterford together, to catch a packet boat to Wales. The twosome were caught before they could leave, and forcibly separated by their families.

The softhearted Lady Betty allowed Eleanor and Sarah a final goodbye, and during the meeting the pair formulated another plan for escape. Eleanor ran away again, straight to Sarah's, where Sarah's faithful servant Mary Caryll helped hide Eleanor in a cupboard.

Despite pressure from family and friends, Sarah maintained that she meant to "live and die with Miss Butler."[5] Eleanor's family was furious, and ten days of negotiations between them commenced, until finally, and without any explanation, Eleanor's father arranged for the women to leave together.

On May 4, 1778, the Ladies set out together for Wales. They remained in Waterford for four days, waiting for the vagaries of maritime travel to sort out, and on May 9, 1778, the Ladies left Ireland, never to return.

Their early travels were recorded by Sarah in her journal titled *An Account of a Journey in Wales, Perform'd in May 1778 by Two Fugitive Ladies, And Dedicated to Her most tenderly Beloved Companion By The Author.* The journal notes the Ladies' first visit to Llangollen on May 25, 1778. Sarah describes it as a "pretty village on the river Dee" but indicates no other opinions on the place that would become their home and with which they would become indelibly linked.

The Ladies meant to settle in England, but the successive and unexpected deaths of Sir William and Lady Betty threw into sharp relief the reality of the Ladies' financial situation. They had a £200 annuity from Eleanor's father and a meager £80 from Lady Betty's daughter Sarah Tighe, who had a fondness for the Ladies.

It seems the Ladies originally settled in Llangollen in 1779, before finally renting the two-story cottage that they christened Plas Newydd, Welsh for "new hall."

Luckily for the Ladies, the local gentry accepted them despite their unconventional living arrangement. This was thanks in large part to Anne Hill-Trevor, Lady Dungannon, a friend of Lady

Betty's, whose embrace of the Ladies paved the way for the rest of the local gentry to befriend them.

By 1789 Sarah and Eleanor's letters are full of descriptions of busy social calendars. And despite many reports to the contrary, they maintained a line of communication with many family members, some of whom offered financial assistance, while others even visited. They had a wide circle of local friends, and socialized with many important thinkers, writers, and politicians of their time.

The Ladies' beloved and faithful servant Mary Caryll died in 1809. Eleanor died in 1829, and Sarah followed in 1831. The three are buried together at St. Collen's Church in Llangollen.

THE LADIES' AFTERLIFE

The Ladies have long been embraced as queer icons. The unusual nature of their lives means that they were much discussed during and after their lifetimes.

The Ladies were acutely aware of the importance of their public reputation. They knew public acceptance was key to their families financially supporting them in their unconventional arrangement. And to be publicly accepted, the Ladies had to maintain that their association was friendship, rather than a sexual relationship.

Unlike Anne Damer and Anne Lister, the Ladies considered legal action when faced with printed accusations of lesbianism. They even consulted a lawyer. Their very existence depended on strict control of their public image.

Perhaps this is one reason the Ladies were so resistant to having their portrait made. Only one image drawn from life exists of the Ladies. It is a watercolor that Mary Parker, later Lady Leighton, made on a visit with her mother. This image is the basis for the Ladies' future visual legacy. [Figure 17]

Like Anne Lister, the Ladies developed their own distinct style. They both wore their hair cropped short and favored black riding habits and top hats when out and about. This choice to dress as they pleased was another way to assert their individuality.

They were visited by writers like Anna Seward, William Wordsworth, Percy Shelley, and Lord Byron. The Ladies encouraged their visitors to write poems inspired by their visits. These poems are fascinating additions to the debate about how the Ladies were received by their contemporaries. The poems and other writings produced by visitors to Llangollen played an important role in the mythologizing of the Ladies and their relationship.

William Wordsworth's poem To the Lady E. B. and Hon. Miss P. Composed in the Grounds of Plas Newydd, near Llangollen, 1824

A stream, to mingle with your favorite Dee,
Along the Vale of Meditation flows;
In Nature's face the expression of repose;
Or haply there some pious hermit chose
To live and die, the peace of heaven his aim;
To whom the wild, sequestered region owes,

At this late day, its sanctifying name,
Glyn Cafaillgaroch, in the Cambrian Tongue,
In ours, the Vale of Friendship, let this spot
Be named, where, faithful to a low-roofed cot,
On Deva's banks ye have abode so long;
Sisters in love, a love allowed to climb,
Even on this earth, above the reach of time!

In his flattering poem, Wordsworth is careful to situate the Ladies in their appropriate place of honor, both historically and geographically. He also softens the truth of their cohabitation, ascribing their unusual choice to the love of sisters.

The Ladies and questions surrounding their sexuality were treated differently than were contemporary assumed lesbians, like Anne Damer. While Damer was the subject of a number of satirical images, most notably *The Damerian Apollo*, the Ladies arranged for and encouraged their many illustrious visitors to write poetry inspired by their visits to Plas Newydd. The Ladies were careful to influence how they were perceived by cultivating friendships and encouraging prestigious visitors, keeping them in control of their public narrative in a fascinating, and important, way.

WERE THE LADIES LESBIANS?

Ever since the Ladies' elopement, there has been debate about the sexual nature of their relationship, one that has continued throughout years of scholarship.

The Ladies have long been considered in the tradition of "romantic friendship." This is due in large part to Elizabeth Mavor's seminal work *The Ladies of Llangollen: A Study in Romantic Friendship* (1971). Mavor cites Sarah Tighe's contemporary letter from immediately after the Ladies' first attempt at elopement: "The runaways are caught and we shall soon see our amiable friend [Ponsonby] again whose conduct, although has an appearance of imprudence, is I am sure void of serious impropriety. There were no gentlemen involved, nor does it appear more than a scheme of Romantic Friendship."

Mavor joins Lillian Faderman in the tradition of academics who insist that these female friendships were socially acceptable and almost certainly physically chaste.

There is another, very different school of thought that situates the Ladies firmly in the middle of the gay and lesbian liberation movement. Jeanette H. Foster's *Sex Variant Women in Literature* (1956) included the Ladies in a chapter on women of whom "persistent rumor or conjectural evidence strongly suggests variance."

What is clear is that the Ladies made unconventional choices that were accepted, if sometimes questioned, by their contemporaries.

Rather than declare them lesbians or any other sexual identity, *queer* seems to fit the Ladies best. As David Halperin notes, "Queer is by definition whatever is at odds with the normal, the legitimate, the dominant." The Ladies certainly fit within that tradition. They courted respectability while also refusing to conform to the expected.

CONCLUSION

The presence of so many queer women in the Regency world gives us a hint at the answer to the age-old question of why the Regency continues to fascinate and delight so many generations.

We think of the Regency as strictly governed by a set of social rules, and queer women would seem to fall outside those carefully constructed boundaries. However, Anne Damer, Anne Lister, the Ladies of Llangollen, and the many women they loved tell us otherwise. They show us that not only did queer people exist in the Regency, but they found communities that accepted them and made full, happy lives for themselves.

The queer women in this chapter did not exist in isolation. Anne Lister visited the Ladies at Plas Newydd, admiring their "rustic library"[6] and admitting, "I am interested about these two ladies very much."[7] The Ladies were also connected to Anne Damer through their mutual friend Anna Seward, a poet of renown who enjoyed her own close relationships with women.

Indeed, the same names show up again and again in studies of lesbianism in the nineteenth century, indicating once again that even if the network was unofficial it very much existed, tying the queer women of the nineteenth century to one another through bonds of friendship and love.

The Regency was a period of immense change politically, artistically, and culturally. Amid that upheaval, queer people not only existed but thrived. Their stories, in all their complicated, messy glory, can teach us so much. They help us better understand the complicated line women walked between acceptable and unacceptable social behavior, and how, if they were determined enough, they could carve out a life on their own terms, loving and living as they chose.

Recommended Reading/Viewing

Beynon, John, and Caroline Gonda. *Lesbian Dames: Sapphism in the Long Eighteenth Century*. Routledge, 2010.

Brideoak, Fiona. *The Ladies of Llangollen: Desire, Indeterminacy, and the Legacies of Criticism*. Bucknell University Press, 2017.

Castle, Terry. *The Apparitional Lesbian: Female Homosexuality and Modern Culture*. Columbia University Press, 1993.

Donoghue, Emma. *Passions Between Women: British Lesbian Culture 1668–1801*. Bello, 2014.

Faderman, Lillian. *Surpassing the Love of Men: Romantic Friendship and Love Between Women from the Renaissance to the Present*. Harper, 1998.

Gentleman Jack (television series). HBO, 2019.

Haggerty, George. *Unnatural Affections: Women and Fiction in the Later Eighteenth Century*. Indiana University Press, 1998.

Moore, Lisa. *Dangerous Intimacies: Toward a Sapphic History of the British Novel*. Duke University Press, 1997.

Oram, Alison, and Annmarie Turnbull. *The Lesbian History Sourcebook: Love and Sex Between Women in Britain from 1780 to 1970*. Routledge, 2013.

Vivincus, Martha. *Intimate Friends: Women Who Loved Women 1778–1982*. University of Chicago Press, 2006.

Wahl, Elizabeth. *Invisible Relations: Representations of Female Intimacy in the Age of Enlightenment*. Stanford University Press, 1999.

Whitbread, Helena. *I Know My Own Heart: The Diaries of Anne Lister, 1791–1840*. New York University Press, 1992.

[Figure 14] Daniel Gardner.
The Three Witches from Macbeth (Georgiana, Duchess of Devonshire; Elizabeth Lamb, Viscountess Melbourne; and Anne Seymour Damer). 1775.
(© National Portrait Gallery, London)

[Figure 15] *The Damerian Apollo.*
Published 1789 by William Holland. British Museum.
(Courtesy of The Lewis Walpole Library, Yale University)

[Figure 16] Richard Cosway. *Untitled, Anne Damer and Mary Berry.*
Sketch circa late eighteenth century.
Lewis Walpole Library, Yale University.
(Courtesy of The Lewis Walpole Library, Yale University)

[Figure 17] Richard James Lane, after Mary Parker. *The Ladies of Llangollen*. Circa 1830. National Portrait Gallery. *(The Rt. Hon. Lady Eleanor Butler and Miss Ponsonby, 'The Ladies of Llangollen,' after 1831 [litho], English School [19th century]/New York Public Library, USA/Bridgeman Images.)*

CHAPTER SEVEN

Historical Accuracy and Regency England

In July 2019 Netflix and Shonda Rhimes announced the cast for the upcoming adaptation of the much-loved Regency-set romance series by Julia Quinn, The Bridgertons. Eight books following eight in-alphabetical-order siblings, in which each one falls in love and gets a happy ending. The bickering but loving siblings and their mother are a beloved family in the romance community. The news that Shonda Rhimes and Netflix would be adapting the books into an eight-episode series was met with extreme excitement.

Julie Andrews was announced as the voice of Lady Whistledown, the anonymous gossip columnist who clues the reader into the behind-the-scenes drama surrounding the Bridgertons and their social circle. This casting was widely celebrated.

The issue came with the announcement of Regé-Jean Page as Simon Basset, the Duke of Hastings. Page is a British-Zimbabwean actor and fans took to social media, littering author Julia Quinn's casting announcement posts with comments decrying "politically correct casting" and bemoaning a lack of "historical accuracy."

Page was not the only Black actor cast in the series. Golda Rosheuvel, a Black British actress, was cast as Queen Charlotte. This casting is an accurate reflection of real life, as Queen Charlotte was directly descended from Margarita de Castro e Souza, a fifteenth-century Portuguese noblewoman who was herself a descendant of Alfonso III and his mistress Madragana from the thirteenth century.

And Page as Simon Basset, a duke, was not without his own historical precedent. Dido Elizabeth Belle, born to an enslaved woman and an Englishman, was raised in England by her uncle Lord Mansfield, alongside her cousin Lady Elizabeth Murray. Contemporary letters indicate that Dido was very much a part of her aristocratic family, to some visitors' consternation.

And Dido wasn't alone as she moved among the upper classes in nineteenth-century England. By the 1780s it was common practice for African leaders to send their sons to England for education, just as they had done with their trading partners in Spain and Portugal before.

The question of diversity and historical accuracy has long roiled the romance community, and the controversy around the Bridgertons casting brought it to the forefront of a community dealing with its own history of systemic racism.

Most Regency romance novels written in the twenty-first century feature entirely white casts of characters. Most Regency-set period movies and TV shows similarly show only white faces on screen. Historical evidence tells us this is a reflection not of the truth, but rather of a modern fantasy that whitewashes history. In actuality, romance novels and plays written in the nineteenth century often featured characters of color.

The Queen of the Regency Novel Jane Austen featured a West Indian heiress, Miss Lambe, in her unfinished novel *Sanditon*. Miss Lambe is a largely unspeaking role, but she's certainly there on the page, existing with the white heiresses she attends school alongside. The schoolmistress Mrs. Griffiths is not prejudiced against Miss Lambe; quite the opposite, as we are informed that Miss Lambe is sickly and under the constant care of a physician and must have the best accommodations, even compared with the white Beaufort sisters also under Mrs. Griffiths's care.

Austen is not alone. There are many more examples of classic Regency authors who included characters of color, including Maria Edgeworth and Charlotte Dacre.

DIDO ELIZABETH BELLE

One of the most famous of Regency women of color today and in her own time is Dido Elizabeth Belle, the mixed-race woman who lived among the aristocracy of the late eighteenth and early nineteenth centuries, immortalized in Amma Asante's 2013 film *Belle.*

Dido Elizabeth Belle was born in 1761 to Admiral Sir John Lindsay and an enslaved woman named Maria Belle. Dido was not the only mixed-race child Lindsay fathered, but she appears to be the only one taken in and raised by his family. According to colonial laws, she was born into slavery, but it seems very likely that Dido never lived as an enslaved person. Her uncle Lord Mansfield officially granted her her freedom in his will, written in 1782 and in effect upon his death in 1793.

It appears that Dido was born in England, but she was not baptized until the age of five at St. George's Church in Bloomsbury. Lindsay was not present, nor did he give the child his name. But he did provide for Dido and her mother's futures in other very important ways. In 1773 Lindsay arranged for a parcel of land he owned in Pensacola, Florida, to be transferred to Maria Belle with the caveat that she build a house on the property.

Aware that his career and lifestyle made raising a child impossible, Lindsay placed Dido in the care of his uncle William Murray, first Earl of Mansfield. Lord Mansfield was already looking after another great-niece, Elizabeth Murray, who had come to stay with him after the death of her mother in 1766.

Lord Mansfield and his wife, Elizabeth, raised the girls together.

There is a famous portrait of the pair traditionally attributed to Johan Zoffany, though that attribution has recently been questioned and it has been reattributed to Scottish portraitist David Martin. [Figure 18] The portrait, generally dated around 1779, shows Dido and Elizabeth standing on the grounds of Kenwood House where they were raised. Dido is dressed in a white satin gown accompanied by a turban bedecked in diamonds and an ostrich feather, the height of fashion at the time. In her arm she cradles a bowl of fruit, grapes spilling over the edge. Her other hand is raised to her face, one delicate finger resting on her cheek as a mischievous grin tugs at her lips. A luxurious strand of pearls encircles her neck, while two large pearls hang from her ears. Evocatively, a gauzy blue scarf trails behind her, lifted up by a passing wind.

Elizabeth wears a pale-pink dress with lace details along the cuffs and stomacher, a double strand of pearls around her neck and flowers in her hair. In one hand she holds an open book; her other hand reaches out and holds on to Dido's.

It is this affectionate gesture that has arrested historians' attentions for years.

Even if Dido had been brought into the house as an attendant or paid companion for Elizabeth, the portrait shows that by 1779, the pair had a very different relationship. They are both richly dressed, both painted with detail and care and traditional symbols of femininity. The equal way they are treated stands in marked contrast with other nineteenth-century portraits featuring people of color, where they are often shown as exotic servants.

Dido and Elizabeth received very different inheritances from their uncle upon his death. While Dido was granted her freedom, £500, and a £100 annuity for the rest of her life, Elizabeth was left £10,000. Of course, Elizabeth was the legitimate child of Lord Mansfield's nephew, while Dido was illegitimate, which in some ways accounts for part of the discrepancy.

Dido's illegitimacy was delicately mentioned in her father's obituary from 1788, where she is described as his "natural daughter."[1] The obituary also highlights Dido's place of importance in her adopted family, noting that her "amiable disposition and accomplishments have gained her the highest respect from all relations and visitants."[2]

Elizabeth married George Finch-Hatton in 1785; they had two sons and a daughter. She died in 1825.

Dido married John Davinier, a Frenchman, in 1793. They had twin sons, Charles and John, in 1795, and another son, William Thomas, in 1802. Dido died just three years later, in 1805.

In the portrait Dido and Elizabeth are shown as equals, with none of the traditional markers that indicate a difference in their stations to the viewer—other than the color of their skin. But outside the carefully painted canvas they and their descendants had different lives.

Elizabeth's son became the tenth Earl of Winchelsea while two of Dido's sons were employed by the East India Company. This was a respectable establishment, but it was an employer nonetheless. Dido's children had to work for the rest of their lives, while Elizabeth's enjoyed a much more rarefied life.

Dido herself often worked as a secretary for Lord Mansfield as he served as lord chief justice of the King's Bench. Widely considered one of the most powerful jurists of his time, he held in *Somerset v. Stewart* in 1772 that slavery was unsupported by common law in England. Mansfield ruled on several cases relating to slavery, and his judgments have been carefully parsed by historians for any hint of Dido's influence.

Evidence tells us that Dido was a beloved family member, respected and fully integrated into the lives of her white relatives. Dido and her sons should be considered as part of the (recently fully examined) phenomenon of mixed-race families who immigrated to England during the long eighteenth century and into the early nineteenth. While the majority of white men who fathered children with women of color during this time did little or nothing to care for their children, there is a growing body of evidence of fathers who actually took an active interest in these mixed-race children, and in some cases brought them back to England to be educated and live among their white family.

In his book *Children of Uncertain Fortune: Mixed-Race Jamaicans in Britain and the Atlantic Family, 1733–1833*, Daniel Livesay breaks the development of popular opinion about mixed-race families into four unique stages, each intimately tied to the slave trade. He starts with the enslaved uprising known as Tacky's Revolt in Jamaica, which led to a tightening of the power structures in the Caribbean. Next, in the 1760s, the growing abolition movement led to questions about family structures and immigration of mixed-race children to England. After this shift, a wave of bad publicity for mixed-race people came in the 1780s as concerns moved to inheritance and destabilization of the norm. Finally, Livesay points to a growing disdain after the Haitian Revolution of 1791 for rich, illegitimate mixed-race people, who were seen as imposters and therefore excluded from high society. Dido, however, does not fit into any of these four stages. She arrived in England at the very beginning of Livesay's stage one, and her life in England spans the rest of them.

Yet it is clear that Dido and her fellow mixed-race inhabitants of the early nineteenth century were a visual reminder of the very real and moral question of slavery and abolition. Historians tiptoe around the question of Dido and her influence on Lord Mansfield and his legal decisions. And it's certainly not black-and-white. There are shades of gray. But it is difficult to reconcile Dido's place in her family with some of Lord Mansfield's legal rulings and writings.

Dido seems to exist firmly in what Livesay calls the "Atlantic family": that complex web of relationships formed by families with joint European and African ancestries. But she has been discounted by historians of the Regency as too unique to study or include in larger grapplings with the era.

But this was an era of huge change, especially for the family unit.

It is undeniable that Dido gave a face to these larger moral and existential questions for her family and friends. She lived and moved among them as life- and history-altering questions were decided by those she was closest to.

We have no written record of Dido's thoughts or feelings. The main source of information on her life is her uncle Lord Mansfield and the brief notes he jotted down about her. The other source is the visitors to Kenwood House who filtered their views of Dido through their own (often prejudiced) lenses. American visitors were particularly surprised at the familiar way Dido was treated by the family, highlighting the difference between American and British attitudes toward people of color as debates around abolition and the morality of slavery raged. Thomas Hutchinson, captain general and governor in chief of Massachusetts Bay, visited Kenwood House and wrote:

> A Black came in after dinner and sat with the ladies and after coffee, walked with the company in the gardens, one of the young ladies having her arm within the other. She had a very high cap and her wool was much frizzled in her neck, but not enough to answer the large curls now in fashion. She is neither handsome nor genteel—pert enough. [They call] her Dido, which I suppose is all the name she has. He knows he has been reproached for showing fondness for her—I dare say not criminal.[3]

We have no record of how Dido felt about such visitors and scrutiny. What we do have is the portrait—the clearest indication of her privileged place beside her cousin.

The fictionalized version of Dido's life, the 2013 film *Belle* directed by Amma Asante, compresses many of the historical events that took place during Dido's life that led to the outlawing of slavery in England. The film imagines Dido at the center of the debate as her uncle decides on the case of *Gregson v. Gilbert*. The case was sparked by the Zong massacre, when the crew of a British slave ship murdered 130 slaves by throwing them overboard, supposedly because they had run out of water but in reality to cash in on the insurance policies that had been taken out on the slaves as cargo. The ruling, presided over by Lord Mansfield, found that the deliberate killing of slaves was in some instances lawful. But after the trial new evidence came to light that there had been rain on the second day of the murders, leading to a retrial.

In the film *Belle*, the famous portrait of Dido and Elizabeth is unveiled right before Lord Mansfield is due to rule on *Gregson v. Gilbert*. Dido sees the painting through a window as the artist unveils it to Lord Mansfield. The music swells as Dido and her uncle share a significant glance.

"It will hang at Kenwood," he tells her.

"It will?" she asks.

"Why should that surprise you?"

"Why should it not?"

The discussion that follows shows that Dido is very aware of her complicated place in the world. She doesn't see herself in the stories of slaves she hears; nor does she belong in high society. But she also knows the importance she has for her uncle (whom she calls Papa in the film) and speaks a line that gets to the heart of Dido's extraordinary life: "When it comes to the matters you believe in, society is inconsequential. You break every rule when it matters enough, Papa. I am the evidence. This painting is the evidence."[4]

MARY SEACOLE

Many of us learned in school about Florence Nightingale, known as the founder of modern nursing due to her heroic actions during the Crimean War.

But Florence had a colleague, a Jamaican-Scottish woman named Mary Seacole, who was also famous for her nursing heroics during the war, heroics she detailed in the first autobiography published by a Black woman in England, in 1857. After her death in 1881, Mary's fame was far surpassed by Florence Nightingale's, and she began to fade from memory.

Luckily, in the 1980s there came a renewed interest in Mary with a new edition of her bestselling autobiography *Wonderful Adventures of Mrs. Seacole in Many Lands* (1984). In 2005 the two-hundredth anniversary of Mary's birth was celebrated with the unveiling of a newly discovered portrait at the National Portrait Gallery. [Figure 19]

But the rediscovery and celebration of Mary's lifework has not been without its detractors, who, just like those angry about the Bridgertons casting, call foul on the supposed "politically correct" insertion of people of color into the historical record. In 2013 British education secretary Michael Gove drew the ire of historians and the public when he attempted to remove Mary Seacole from the national curriculum. Gove and his supporters insisted that Mary's contributions had been overblown, somehow at the expense of Florence Nightingale, and that removing her from the curriculum would give students more time to study Winston Churchill.

This decision was rightly and roundly denounced, and thirty-five thousand people signed a petition demanding that Mary remain in the teaching materials on Victorian Britain, resulting in a defensive statement from the Department of Education: "Previous media reports that Mary Seacole was not included in the new National Curriculum were speculation. We have never said that Mary Seacole would not be a part of the Curriculum."[5]

~~

Mary Jane Grant was born in 1805 in Kingston, Jamaica. Her father, James Grant, was a Scottish soldier and her mother was a Jamaican woman who ran a boardinghouse and was well known as a "doctress." Mary was taken with her mother's work from a young age.

> I was so spoiled by my kind patroness that, but for being frequently with my mother, I might very likely have grown up idle and useless. But I saw so much of her, and of her patients, that the ambition to become a doctress early took firm root in my mind; and I was very young when I began to make use of the little knowledge I had acquired from watching my mother, upon a great sufferer—my doll... So I also made good use of my dumb companion and confidante; and whatever disease was most prevalent in Kingston, be sure my poor doll soon contracted it. I have had many medical triumphs in later days, and saved some valuable lives; but I really think that few have given me more real gratification

> than the rewarding glow of health which my fancy used to picture stealing over my patient's waxen face after long and precarious illness.[6]

One of the many ways Mary's detractors have tried to undermine her right to appear in the historical record is by questioning her medical expertise, especially compared with the more traditionally trained Florence Nightingale.

What is clear from Mary's memoir is that she was carefully trained and always eager to learn new nursing techniques. She took her profession seriously.

She was also very aware of the prejudices she would and did face due to her skin color. On a visit to England in 1821 she experienced racial prejudice, which stayed with her for the rest of her life. "Strangely enough, some of the most vivid of my recollections are the efforts of the London street-boys to poke fun at my and my companion's complexion."[7]

On November 10, 1836, Mary married Edwin Horatio Hamilton Seacole in Kingston, Jamaica. Seacole was a godson (and rumored illegitimate son) of Admiral Horatio Nelson. Unfortunately, Seacole was often ill, and Mary spent much of their marriage nursing him. He died in 1844, leaving Mary a widow. Soon after, Mary's mother also died.

After her mother's death, Mary took over her boardinghouse, Blundell Hall. During the cholera outbreak of 1850, which killed over thirty-two thousand Jamaicans, Mary nursed many back to health and received public acclaim for her efforts.

Mary believed that cholera had come to the island by a steamer ship from New Orleans. She was right about contagion theory and would use what she had learned in Jamaica during future outbreaks.

In 1851 Mary traveled to Cruces, Panama, to join her half brother, who had opened the Independent Hotel. Almost immediately upon her arrival she was faced with a new cholera outbreak. Mary went right to work taking care of patients and establishing her reputation as an effective nurse. "There was no doctor in Cruces; the nearest approach to one was a little timid dentist, who was there by accident, and who refused to prescribe for the sufferer, and I was obliged to do my best. Selecting from my medicine chest—I never travel anywhere without it—what I deemed necessary, I went hastily to the patient, and at once adopted the remedies I considered fit. It was a very obstinate case, but by dint of mustard emetics, warm fomentations, mustard plasters on the stomach and the back, and calomel, at first in large then in gradually smaller doses, I succeeded in saving my first cholera patient in Cruces."[8]

Mary herself even fell sick with cholera due to her nursing patients through the disease, but she recovered quickly. In 1852 she opened her own hotel, the British Hotel, but she soon packed up and moved to Gorgona, Panama, where she opened a women-only boardinghouse.

In 1854 Mary turned her attention to the worsening situation with the Crimean War. Hundreds of soldiers were dying, not due to fighting, but due to diseases like cholera. Florence Nightingale was approached to form a unit of nurses to be sent to Turkey to help with the war effort.

Mary was determined to join this contingent, but she was turned away when she applied at the War Office.

> Now, I am not for a single instant going to blame the authorities who would not listen to the offer of a motherly yellow woman to go to the Crimea and nurse her "sons" there, suffering from cholera, diarrhea, and a host of lesser ills. In my country, where people know our use, it would have been different; but here it was natural enough—although I had references, and other voices spoke for me—that they should laugh, good-naturedly enough, at my offer.[9]

Mary was not deterred by the racism she faced. She next applied directly to Florence Nightingale's elite force of nurses, but was once again turned away. Mary was much more affected by this setback, writing, "Doubts and suspicions arose in my heart for the first and last time, thank Heaven. Was it possible that American prejudices against colour had some root here? Did these ladies shrink from accepting my aid because my blood flowed beneath a somewhat duskier skin than theirs? Tears streamed down my foolish cheeks, as I stood in the fast thinning streets; tears of grief that any should doubt my motives—that Heaven should deny me the opportunity that I sought."[10]

Despite this heartbreak and setback, Mary was not dissuaded. She decided to travel to Turkey with her new business partner Thomas Day to reopen the British Hotel. When Mary arrived in Constantinople she did finally meet with Florence Nightingale.

While Nightingale provided Mary with a bed for the night, she did not join Nightingale's nurses.

Instead Mary continued to travel and settled on the road between Balaclava and the British camp near Sevastopol. The new British Hotel was opened in 1855. There Mary served meals and nursed wounded soldiers. She often went out into battlefields, selling goods and ministering to wounds in the field.

After the war ended, Mary had to shut down her business at a loss. She traveled back to England completely destitute. She was feted by soldiers but had to declare bankruptcy in 1856.

Mary's difficulties were widely reported and fund-raising efforts were undertaken by grateful soldiers. In 1857 the Seacole Fund Grand Military Festival was held at the Royal Surrey Gardens to raise funds for Mary. It was attended by a crowd of forty thousand, but the Royal Surrey Gardens company was having financial difficulties of their own, so Mary only received £57.

In 1860 Mary returned to Jamaica, where she converted to Catholicism. Her money problems persisted and another fund was raised. Ten years later she returned to London, where she once again was received with accolades. She was appointed official masseuse to Alexandra, the Princess of Wales, who suffered from rheumatism.

Mary died at her home in London in 1888. Despite her difficulties with money for most of her life, she left behind an estate of over £2,500.

Mary took careful pains to ensure that her extraordinary life and work would be remembered by future generations when she dictated her memoir to an anonymous editor in 1857. She left behind a record of what it was like to live as a Black woman during the nineteenth century, giving us insight into such disparate worlds as Jamaica, Panama, England, and Turkey.

Mary faced prejudice head-on. Her memoirs are littered with moments where she was discriminated against or treated poorly due to the color of her skin, but Mary never let it stop her from her life's mission, learned at her mother's knee, of helping the sick.

PRINCESS CARABOO

Given everything we have learned about prejudices against people of color in Regency England, it's particularly interesting to consider the case of Mary Baker, otherwise known as Princess Caraboo. Mary Baker was a poor English woman who invented the persona of a foreign-born princess. She was successful in her deception for a few months.

How and why did a poor English girl choose to disguise herself as a foreign-born princess if, as we are told, there were no people of color in Regency England?

Almost everything we know about Mary Baker comes from her contemporaneous biographer John Mathew Gutch, who wrote a narrative account of the hoax and published it in 1817, shortly after Mary Baker's true identity was revealed.

The story starts with the supposed Princess Caraboo appearing in the Gloucestershire village of Almondsbury on April 3, 1817. She was dressed in black, and appeared not to speak English, instead using hand gestures and an unknown language to communicate. She was also in possession of two counterfeit coins, a serious offense.

Princess Caraboo was taken to the county magistrate Samuel Worrall and his American-born wife, Elizabeth, for examination. Aside from speaking another language, Princess Caraboo had displayed other indications that she might be foreign-born. She excitedly recognized a painting of a pineapple and identified it using the word *ananas*, which means "pineapple" in several indigenous languages. She also bowed her head and prayed in her unknown language before and after eating, and before sleeping on the floor despite the presence of a good bed in her room.

No one knew what to do with Princess Caraboo so she was sent to the mayor of Bristol, who sent her to St. Peter's Hospital for examination as required by law. While there, a Portuguese sailor named Manuel Eynesso contacted the authorities, claiming to speak Princess Caraboo's language. After meeting with her, he told "her" story of how she was from a small island nation of Javasu and had been captured by pirates, whom she had escaped from by jumping overboard and swimming to safety in England.

The Worralls, believing Princess Caraboo was a highborn foreign woman who had had a terrible ordeal at the hands of pirates, took her into their home. There she received visiting dignitaries who were fascinated by her story. Princess Caraboo demonstrated her abilities for her visitors, showing them her skill with a bow and arrow and, perhaps more scandalously, swimming naked in the lake.

The press was so intrigued by Princess Caraboo's story that it was shared widely, along with accompanying portraits of the princess in her exotic garb. It was upon seeing Princess Caraboo's painting in the *Bristol Journal* that a boardinghouse keeper named Mrs. Neale instantly recognized the supposed princess as local girl Mary Baker, the daughter of a cobbler.

Princess Caraboo was exposed. The result was widespread mockery of the Worralls for being taken in by Mary Baker's deceit. Still, Mrs. Worrall kindly arranged for Mary Baker to travel to America on June 28, 1817, just a few short months after the entire saga started. Mary was received with excitement in America, where the Princess Caraboo story was well known. She went on a tour of theaters, giving performances as the princess.

In 1824 Mary returned to England, continuing to perform as Princess Caraboo. However, her life took a sad turn; the next time we find her in the historical record she is selling leeches to the Bristol Hospital. Catching the leeches sometimes involved using your own body as bait. Mary died in 1864 and was buried in an unmarked grave.

Gutch's narrative of Mary Baker's time with the Worralls is fascinating. It explains exactly how Mary took cues from the people around her, adapting her behaviors to fulfill their expectations of her as a foreign-born woman. Mary Baker was a poor woman with little to no education. It is telling that despite this, she was still able to successfully mimic a foreigner, and even create a compelling character for her hosts to engage with.

As Gutch points out, Mary Baker was a popular guest of the Worralls who entertained visitors with a wide range of education. Whenever something was pointed out to her as something she would be doing, if she was truly foreign, she simply adapted. Mary

Baker's genius was in taking advantage of everyone underestimating her. It was accepted that she didn't speak English, but as Gutch tells us, she listened while people talked around her and used their information against them.

Mary Baker knew there was more value in her invented Princess Caraboo persona than her real-life status as a poor white English woman. She subverted the contemporary views of women in perhaps the most subversive way possible. A poor, uneducated woman shows us that everything we and her contemporaries think and thought about nineteenth-century women barely scratches the surface of the truth.

CONCLUSION

As Tudor historian Miranda Kaufmann has noted, "History isn't a solid set of facts... it's very much about what questions you ask of the past. If you ask different questions, you get different answers. People weren't asking questions about diversity. Now they are."[11]

We're asking different questions and looking for different stories than we have in the past. This is an exciting time for history as stories that have long languished in the shadows are brought into the light.

The concept of "the Regency" itself is such a loaded one. Technically, it refers to only the ten-year period in England between 1810 and 1820 when George IV ruled as Regent. But how do we divest one historical moment and place from the enormously important context surrounding it?

While the long eighteenth century, ending with the distinctive Georgian era in England, dragged into the start of the new era, it collided with the so-called Regency in the early aughts of the 1800s.

Meanwhile in France, we were squarely in the Napoleonic era, heading fast toward the Napoleonic Wars.

The former colonies were settling into the United States after gaining their independence, with their attention shifting toward expansion and the continuing genocide of the indigenous population to make way for European and Christian settlers.

In China the population had doubled (similar to the population growth that occurred in the nineteenth century in Europe). The ports were opened to Western trade and missionaries after a series of military losses to European forces.

If we separate England's Regency from its global context we miss out on so much of the story. We also do a disservice to the people of the early nineteenth century who certainly considered themselves as global citizens, communicating with each other despite distance.

The many remarkable women of the larger nineteenth century world were certainly known of and discussed in the ballrooms and sitting rooms of Regency England. Some of them even inhabited those very ballrooms, forcing us to reexamine our ideas about who and what was accepted, and why.

This book is from a Western perspective, engaging with how England and concepts of Englishness changed contemporaneously and historically. There is no denying the overwhelming whiteness of the Regency in popular imagination. This seems unquestionably tied to the tokenization of the few people of color living in

England who left behind records of their existence. Should we further erase them due to their scarcity?

Or should we contend with their existence and the truth of people of color in England during the nineteenth century? It's not an easy or simple story, and it's certainly not a monolith. We must allow for the many varied hues of humanity to exist in history, or we are ignoring evidence in favor of furthering a white supremacist view of history.

Recommended Reading/Viewing

Belle (film). Fox Searchlight Pictures, 2014.

Byrne, Paula. *Belle: The Slave Daughter and the Lord Chief Justice.* HarperCollins, 2014.

Charles, KJ. *Wanted, A Gentleman.* KJC Books, 2017.

Clark, Emily. *The Strange History of the American Quadroon: Free Women of Color in the Revolutionary Atlantic World.* University of North Carolina Press, 2013.

Dalrymple, William. *White Mughals: Love and Betrayal in Eighteenth-Century India.* Penguin Books, 2002.

Gerzina, Gretchen. *Black England: Life Before Emancipation.* Rutgers University Press, 1995.

Hawes, C. J. *Poor Relations: The Making of the Eurasian Community in British India, 1773–1833.* Routledge, 1996.

Livesay, Daniel. *Children of Uncertain Fortunes: Mixed-Race Jamaicans in Britain and the Atlantic Family, 1733–1833.* University of North Carolina Press, 2018.

Riley, Vanessa. *The Bittersweet Bride.* Entangled, 2018.

Riley, Vanessa. *The Bewildered Bride.* Entangled, 2019.

Sebastian, Cat. *A Gentleman Never Keeps Score.* Avon Impulse, 2018.

[Figure 18] Attributed to David Martin. *Portrait of Dido Elizabeth Belle Lindsay and Lady Elizabeth Murray*. Circa 1778. *(Courtesy of Earls of Mansfield, Scone Palace, Perth, Scotland.)*

[Figure 19] Albert Charles Challen. *Mary Seacole*. 1869.
National Portrait Gallery, London.
(© National Portrait Gallery, London)

CHAPTER EIGHT

Educators and Ambassadors

Jewish Women in the Regency

On the evening of Friday, April 14, 1809, the Royal Dukes of Cambridge, Cumberland, and Sussex visited the Great Synagogue in London. The visit was arranged by Abraham Goldsmid, a wealthy Jewish banker, and it was significant enough that famous satirist Thomas Rowlandson immortalized it in not one but two caricatures.

The first pokes fun at the three royal dukes, replacing their heads with cheese and butter (indicating their general uselessness as political movers and shakers and pointing out the role they played as largely ceremonial royal family members with very little actual power). The royal dukes bow to the rabbi and assembled Jewish men behind him, shown dressed in flowing robes with beards to match.

The second drawing shows the interior of the Great Synagogue. While it still features all the stereotypical anti-Semitism that peppers Rowlandson's other drawings of Jews, the majesty of the space cannot be denied. Light filters in from the high windows, illuminating an enormous room, so large it takes five massive chandeliers to light it. The male congregation sits, facing a large podium in the middle upon which the rabbi stands. In the balcony the Jewish women watch behind a screen.

It was reported that after the dukes visited the synagogue they retired to the home of Abraham Goldsmid to enjoy a "sumptuous entertainment [and] grand concert."[1]

Our popular conception of the religion of the aristocratic circles of the Regency defaults to Christian. Almost every Regency romance published by a major publisher features an entirely Christian cast. (One amazing example of a major series featuring Jewish characters in the Regency, The Courier Series by Nita Abrams, is sadly out of print.)

If we include any Jewish people in our storytelling of nineteenth-century England it is usually in the slums of Whitechapel. Whitechapel was a poor neighborhood where many Jews lived. Its name became synonymous with Jack the Ripper and his brutal murders later in the century. Around fifteen thousand Jews lived in England in 1800, with the majority of them in London. Within this group was also a vibrant, active, and wealthy community of Jews living across England.

They faced an interesting dilemma: assimilate or maintain their religious practices even if it meant they would be discriminated against by their fellow aristocrats.

Judith Montefiore and her fellow wealthy Jews in England and America chose education as their tool of choice in fighting anti-Semitism. As an extremely wealthy Jew connected to many of the aristocratic Jewish families around the world, Judith Montefiore understood the unique position she was in as a potential ambassador for her religion. She was not the only woman in that position, and those who were, were highly aware of the impact they might have.

While Judith reigns as the so-called first lady of Anglo-Jewry, there were other remarkable Jewish women in the early nineteenth century who joined her in her mission to advance the reputation of Judaism in the wider world. In examining the role of Judaism in Regency England it is necessary to travel beyond the borders of the English islands. The Jews of Regency England did not live and think in isolation. Through letters and visits, increasingly far-flung Jewish families kept in close contact with one another, even as they moved around the world.

This global network of Jews in the nineteenth century was concerned about and actively working to engender a new reputation for the Jewish people. After centuries of anti-Semitic depictions in fiction, women like Rebecca Gratz pushed back, encouraging

Christian authors to examine their prejudices and do better, while others, like Grace Aguilar and the King sisters, provided their own, uniquely Jewish writings.

JUDITH MONTEFIORE

No discussion of Judaism in the nineteenth century can occur without mentioning Judith Montefiore. Judith, née Cohen, was a prolific writer who kept journals detailing her life and travels, as well as the first published author of an English-language kosher cookbook.

Born in 1784 to a wealthy Ashkenazi Dutch family that had settled in London, Judith was lucky to be raised in a family that privileged education. She learned French, German, Italian, and Hebrew (rare among women of her station). Later in life she learned Arabic. Judith kept careful diaries throughout her life, but sadly only three complete journals survive. The journals are the meticulous, mannered words of a writer with an eye to publication, rather than deeply personal musings, but they offer a wealth of information about Judith and her world.

In 1812 Judith married the ambitious, up-and-coming banker Moses Montefiore. Her sister Hannah had recently married his cousin Nathan Mayer Rothschild, the head of the Rothschild banking family in England. The two marriages strengthened the connections between the families and proved very successful, financially and otherwise. But the match might not have been an obvious one at first. Judith was from an Ashkenazi family, while

Moses's family was Sephardic. Intermarriages were rare, if not unheard of.

Moses Montefiore was a larger-than-life figure, and in understanding what he saw as his life's mission we can truly begin to understand the relationship among Jews around the world during the nineteenth century. Moses Montefiore made a fortune trading on the London Stock Exchange and decided to use that fortune to fully devote himself to his Jewish philanthropic endeavors.

Judith was delighted at her husband's religious devotion and was his complete partner in achieving his goals. She traveled with him to Damascus, Russia, and Israel five times (one trip to Israel was unthinkable for most people, let alone a woman at the time). Judith was acutely aware of the power of philanthropy to help Judaism's reputation, especially among the elite circles she moved in. In her diaries she writes about inviting friends to celebrate Shabbat with her family at their home in Ramsgate, with the clear belief that if they saw the rituals and prayers they would understand both the similarities and the differences in their religions, and perhaps respect would grow.

Judith is also credited as the writer of *The Jewish Manual: or Practical Information in Jewish & Modern Cookery; with a Collection of Valuable Recipes and Hints Relating to the Toilette*, which was anonymously published in 1846. The manual is considered the first English-language kosher cookbook. It reflects Judith's elite status, as it's written for someone with servants, but it also shares tips and tricks for making popular English recipes kosher by replacing lard and eliminating shellfish.

In her introduction Judith writes,

> We hope, therefore, that this unpretending little work may not prove wholly unacceptable, even to those ladies who are not of the Hebrew persuasion, as it will serve as a sequel to the books on cookery previously in their possession, and be the medium of presenting them with numerous receipts for rare and exquisite compositions, which if uncommemorated by the genius of Vatêl, Ude, or Carême, are delicious enough not only to gratify the lovers of good cheer generally, but to merit the unqualified approbation of the most fastidious epicures.[2]

Judith understood that her cookbook was more important than a simple book of recipes and should really be considered as a part of her larger practice of philanthropy. Of course the recipes themselves are important, because they make kosher cooking accessible. (In particular, it's interesting to see Judith take a popular sauce like béchamel and explain that it could never be truly kosher—but then provide a simple substitute recipe.) By normalizing the practice, however, Judith was actually doing something far more radical.

Along with the recipes, Judith includes beauty tips and moralizing paragraphs. Her cookbook fits squarely in the tradition of nineteenth-century etiquette books. In this way Judith positions the young Jewish hostess she is writing for within this tradition as well. Her audience is no different from their Christian counterparts, except for simple dietary modifications.

According to her diaries, Judith was an outgoing and gregarious person who made it a point to befriend people, especially when traveling. She and her husband systematically and intentionally expanded their social circle beyond the Jewish community in London. They socialized with many important thinkers including Thomas Hodgkin, a Quaker doctor who discovered Hodgkin's lymphoma.

After Judith's death in 1862, Moses put her name on everything he could to honor her memory. He also established a rabbinical teaching school at her beloved home of Ramsgate. Thanks to his generosity, the Montefiore name has remained prominent in Jewish history, and Moses himself is frequently lauded as one of the most important Jewish men of nineteenth-century England. Judith is often mentioned as an aside in the greater story of Moses, but her diaries (the few that survive) tell us a much more complex, intertwined story of a couple that grew together in their goals toward the advancement of the Jewish faith.

REBECCA GRATZ, RACHEL LAZARUS, AND JEWISH LITERARY MUSES

Judith Montefiore was not the only Jewish woman of the nineteenth century focused on education and outreach. Indeed, she was joined by a vibrant community of wealthy Jewish women living across the United States. They were an active, engaged group, working hard to codify and provide Jewish education to children, as well as more charitable services. Like Judith, these women inherently understood the dual power of charity and education to secure a respected place for their religion in the popular imagination.

These early American Jewish women also understood the power of art and worked hard to ensure positive portrayals of Jews.

In 1815 Rachel Mordecai Lazarus wrote to Maria Edgeworth to note the anti-Semitism on display in her popular 1812 novel *The Absentee*. (This letter is sometimes incorrectly attributed to Rebecca Gratz.)

Maria responded, and the pair struck up an epistolary friendship that eventually inspired Maria to "write" her wrongs in the 1817 novel *Harrington*, which featured a sympathetic Jewish heroine, Berenice Montenero. Unfortunately, Maria's solution to Berenice's Jewishness and the problem it presented was to have her father reveal at the end of the novel that she wasn't Jewish at all; the hero Harrington can marry her without his family's disapproval and societal censure.

For both Christians and Jews of the nineteenth century, it is clear that the question of marriage, and interfaith marriage in particular, is a deeply important one.

In 1819 Sir Walter Scott published his own answer to the question with his medieval romance, *Ivanhoe*. His Jewish heroine, Rebecca of York, sacrifices her own happiness for that of the Christian heroine Rowena and Christian hero Ivanhoe. Rebecca is in love with Ivanhoe after nursing him back to health, but she steps aside so he may marry Rowena and live happily ever after. (Rebecca's happily ever after isn't worried about or explicated on the page.) Because of this, Scott's Rebecca is often cited as one of the first positive portrayals of a Jewish protagonist in fiction by a Christian writer.

It has long been rumored that Scott based his paragon of virtue on a real woman: Rebecca Gratz.

Indeed, the rumor was so persistent and widely spread that Rebecca herself believed she was the inspiration for the character, writing to her sister-in-law in 1820, "Have you received *Ivanhoe*? When you read it, tell me what you think of my namesake, Rebecca?"[3] There are many superficial similarities between the real Rebecca Gratz and *Ivanhoe*'s Rebecca. Perhaps most important, they both famously remained unmarried, holding their Jewish faith close while living (and perhaps even falling in love) among Christians.

Born into the wealthy Jewish community in Philadelphia in 1781, Rebecca Gratz dedicated her life to charitable work, founding and leading many important institutions like America's first independent Jewish women's charitable society, the first Jewish Sunday school, the Philadelphia Orphan Asylum, and the first Jewish Foster Home in Philadelphia.

One of twelve children, Rebecca spent a good chunk of her life helping her mother nurse her ailing father, and then lived with her three bachelor brothers. Letters indicate that Rebecca fell in love with a Christian man, and chose to remain unmarried rather than convert or enter into an interfaith marriage.

Rebecca was dedicated to improving the reputation of Judaism in elite circles. This meant founding and supporting a number of charitable institutions, as well as helping others do the same.

Rebecca wasn't the only young Jewish woman dedicated to education. The aforementioned epistolary activist Rachel Mordecai Lazarus was as well. Born in Virginia in 1788, she was the eldest girl in a family of thirteen. Her family moved to North Carolina when she was three, making them the only Jewish family in their small town. The family opened a boarding school in 1809, where Rachel was an educator.

As noted, Rachel read a book by her father's favorite author, Maria Edgeworth, *The Absentee* (1812), and was disappointed to see an anti-Semitic portrayal of Jews, particularly in the character of a mean coachman named Mr. Mordicai.

Rachel wrote to Maria Edgeworth, expressing her disappointment:

> Relying on the good sense and candour of Miss Edgeworth I would ask, how it can be that she, who on all other subjects shows such justice and liberality, should on one alone appear biased by prejudice: should even instill that prejudice in the minds of youth! Can my allusion be mistaken? It is to the species of character which where a Jew is introduced is invariably attached to him. Can it be believed that this race of men are by nature mean, avaricious, and unprincipled? Forbid it, mercy.[4]

Both Maria and her father responded to Rachel's letter. Both letters are kind and conciliatory, thanking Rachel for writing and promising amends. But Maria goes a step further. She tells Rachel she is writing a new book to make up for her past mistakes and asks if she might send a copy to her for her perusal when it's done.

SPOTLIGHT ON MARIA EDGEWORTH

Maria Edgeworth is one of the most famous and important Anglo-Irish writers of the nineteenth century. Publicly lauded in her own time, she has also enjoyed a celebrated legacy in death. She wrote novels, children's stories, and educational treatises alone and with her father Richard Lovell Edgeworth and stepmother Honora Sneyd.[5]

Raised by progressive-thinking parents, Maria attended school until she fell ill at fourteen and returned home to be tutored by her father. Richard Lovell Edgeworth fathered twenty-two children in his lifetime, but still paid an enormous amount of attention to his brilliant daughter Maria. The pair worked together on managing the Edgeworthton Estate, where Maria developed her opinions about land management and tenants' rights, as well as coauthoring *Essays on Practical Education* in 1798.

Maria had something in common with Jewish women writers of the time. As an Anglo-Irish writer, Maria was forever trying to rehabilitate the image of the Irish in books like *Castle Rackrent*. But this similarity did not inspire her to any kind of generosity toward Jews in her work, and her early books are littered with anti-Semitism.

In 1809 Maria published her most ambitious book, *Tales of Fashionable Life*, and was paid £1,050, making her the most commercially successful author of her time.

Maria established and maintained friendships with many leading writers in her day including Sir Walter Scott and Sir William Rowan Hamilton, the latter of whom named Maria as an honorary member of the Royal Irish Academy in 1837.

It is particularly important that Maria and Sir Walter Scott maintained such a close friendship, writing to each other often, as they both wrote books featuring Jewish characters, which were received very differently. While Maria got letters like Rachel Lazarus's, encouraging her to rethink her attitude toward Jews,

Scott's Jewish character Rebecca was praised by her own namesake Rebecca Gratz.

(BACK TO RACHEL LAZARUS)

Maria took Rachel Lazarus's criticism to heart and published *Harrington* in 1817, which was her attempt to respond to the criticism in a direct, fictionalized way. In *Harrington* the titular hero falls in love with a young Jewish woman, Berenice Montenero, and has to examine his own and society's anti-Semitism.

Rachel's words of education literally appear in *Harrington*. Maria lifted a passage from one of Rachel's letters and put it into the text, and Rachel was flattered. "It is impossible to feel otherwise than gratified by the confidence so strongly, yet so delicately manifested, by the insertion of a passage from the letter in which I had endeavored to give an idea of their [Jews'] general standing in this country."[6]

But Rachel wasn't completely satisfied with *Harrington* and she couldn't keep her disappointment to herself, writing to Maria, "Let me therefore, without dwelling longer on its many excellences, confess with frankness that in one event I was disappointed. Berenice was not a Jewess."[7] Rachel writes that her father came up with a reason for Maria's decision, that it must have been to make Berenice's father seem even more noble, a reason she accepts.

When Maria responds she admits she didn't have a reason for making Berenice half Jewish and thanks Rachel's father for his generous suggestion.

Their correspondence doesn't end there. The pair exchanged letters for the rest of their lives, and their descendants carried on the tradition afterward. After her death, Rachel's sister Ellen continued writing to Maria, and upon Maria's death to her stepmother and sisters, and so on and so forth. The correspondence between the extended Lazarus family and the Edgeworth family spans 127 years.

The conversation—both real and imagined—between American Jewish women and English writers in the Regency period resulted in those same writers examining their prejudices and making changes to their work. It's particularly interesting to see the different way Jewish women influenced literature, some with purpose, like Rachel Lazarus, and others through simply existing, like Rebecca Gratz.

GRACE AGUILAR

Born in 1816 to Emanuel and Sarah Aguilar, Portuguese Jews who settled in London after fleeing the Portuguese Inquisition, Grace arrived smack-dab in the middle of the Regency. While she's traditionally associated with the Victorian era, Grace is a product of the Regency era. By studying her life and her work we can see how the ideas of the early nineteenth century directly affected the next generation of Jewish thinkers.

Grace was not a healthy child. She suffered from a number of ailments and illnesses, including a bout with measles in 1835 that seriously weakened her overall health. But Grace's diaries and letters show us that she was still an active young woman, traveling with her family, dancing with friends, and learning the piano and harp. All of which would have been expected activities for a young, middle-class Christian woman.

Grace's father served as the parnas (lay leader and administrator) for London's Spanish and Portuguese Synagogue, the oldest temple in London still in continuous use. (Today it is called Bevis Marks Synagogue.) He had his own bout with ill health in 1828, and the family moved from their home in Hackney to the Tavistock and Teignmouth areas of the Devon coast.

Both the Aguilar parents took an active role in educating Grace and her younger brothers, Emanuel and Henry. Grace was raised on stories from Emanuel about the Portuguese Sephardic Jews who escaped the Portuguese Inquisition by pretending to convert to Catholicism but still secretly practicing Judaism, passing this mixed religion on to their children.

It's clear from later writing that Grace was always special. She was a voracious reader and diarist, keeping a diary from the age of seven, which has sadly almost totally been lost. One short volume, giving us a glimpse of twenty-eight-year-old Grace, survives. Along with her insightful thoughts on religion, Grace shares the regular day-to-day activities of a middle-class woman in the nineteenth century. She writes about enjoying dancing and singing and spending time with her friends and family.

Like her contemporaries Judith Montefiore and Rebecca Gratz, Grace believed deeply in the power of education. She was concerned first and foremost with teaching the next generation, and the materials she prepared for her own brothers' religious education were eventually published as *The Spirit of Judaism* in 1842 by Isaac Leeser, editor of the American Jewish periodical *The Occident*.

But Grace was also very interested in educating the wider world about Judaism.

After the family's move to Devon, Grace was removed from the close-knit Jewish community of London and exposed to a much broader Christian world.

What is so fascinating about Grace is that she actively engaged with Christian theology, even attending church regularly. She made a great number of Christian friends and debated them frequently, always honing her arguments about Judaism. In her book *Sabbath Thoughts* she writes, "It is no credit to be firm and steadfast in your own belief if you are ignorant of that of others..."[8]

Grace believed deeply in the power of debate and education to change the world. She also believed in herself. In 1844 she wrote in her diary, "To be known and loved through my writing has been the yearning and the prayer of my secret heart from the earliest period."[9]

Through her publisher Isaac Leeser, Grace "met" Miriam Cohen, a cousin of Rebecca Gratz's who lived in Savannah, Georgia. Grace and Miriam began an important transatlantic epistolary friendship, their correspondence spanning most of Grace's working life. Miriam's husband, Solomon, became Grace's American distributor, and through him Grace's books entered American Jewish classrooms, including those of Rebecca Gratz.

Grace was careful and conscious of her career choices. While she published in popular Jewish journals like the *Voice of Jacob* and the

Jewish Chronicle, she also submitted her work to popular ladies' magazines like *The Keepsake* and *La Belle Assemblée*. In this way she was sure that her distinctly Jewish writing received a wider audience.

Sadly, the ever-sickly Grace never truly recovered from a final bout of measles in 1847. She died on September 16, 1847. Her mother, Sarah, devoted the rest of her life to editing and publishing Grace's work posthumously. She even kept writing to Miriam Cohen, maintaining the friendship across oceans and generations.

REBECCA SOLOMON

Like Grace Aguilar, Rebecca Solomon is generally considered a part of the Victorian era. However, because she was one of the first professional Jewish women artists in England, we would be remiss to forget her in this book.

Born in 1832, she was raised in the world that the women of the Regency helped to create. Like many other female artists of the nineteenth century, Rebecca was lucky enough to be born into an artistic family. She was the seventh child of Meyer and Kate Solomon, who emigrated from Germany to England with their family in the late eighteenth century.

The Solomons were a very wealthy manufacturing family who continued to enjoy success upon their arrival in London. The family was so accepted that Meyer was the first Jewish person honored with the Freedom of the City of London, a recognition awarded to those who have made great advancements in their career.

Three of the Solomon children became artists. Brothers

Abraham and Simeon trained at the Royal Academy of Arts Schools, while Rebecca, a woman and therefore not accepted at the prestigious institution, trained at the Spitalfields School of Design.

After studying at Spitalfields, Rebecca worked in the studios of important Pre-Raphaelite artists John Everett Millais and Edward Burne-Jones. Her early work fits neatly into the visual world of Victorian painting, with critics noting her humanizing touch.

In the 1850s Rebecca turned to classical and historical painting, the most prestigious and critically valued art one could produce at the time. It's also the kind of art almost exclusively associated with male artists.

Very few of Rebecca's original paintings survive. But she was so popular that many of them were published as engravings in newspapers like the *Illustrated London News*, and we can see her work there.

There are many remarkable things about Rebecca Solomon's career, but the themes she returned to again and again are her enduring legacy. Rebecca's art rarely included overtly Jewish themes or subjects (unless she was painting her own family members). Instead Rebecca, like her fellow Jewish women of the nineteenth century, subtly wove the tenets of Judaism through all of her art, focusing on women, children, and minorities and their struggles.

She successfully exhibited at the Royal Academy and in 1859 joined a group of thirty-eight women artists who petitioned for the Royal Academy Schools to admit women.

Rebecca remained unmarried her whole life and lived with her brothers, first Abraham and then Simeon, as was tradition for unmarried Jewish women at the time. It's not surprising then that

Rebecca's career and reputation were very much tied to those of her siblings. Simeon, in particular, was a popular society figure with a flamboyant lifestyle. This seems to have led to rumors of Rebecca embracing a more exciting lifestyle, including periods of heavy drinking. However, she remained an observant Jew her whole life and an active member of the Jewish community.

Rebecca died in 1886, after being hit by a hansom cab. She left behind a collection of artwork that provides us a unique viewpoint into the time period.

CHARLOTTE DACRE AND SOPHIA KING

There is less biographical information available about Charlotte Dacre and her sister Sophia King than any of the other women featured in this chapter. But that lack of material makes them no less fascinating or important.

Charlotte was born around 1772 to Jacob Rey (better known as John King) and Deborah Lara. We have no date for Sophia's birth. John was a self-made banker and well-known radical thinker. He divorced his first wife under Jewish law in 1785 to marry the widowed Countess of Lanesborough (who was Christian). We don't know how this step up in social status affected Charlotte and Sophia, but the theme of women being abandoned by men appears frequently in their work.

John was also infamous for an episode involving Mary Robinson, author and onetime mistress to George IV. While his job as a banker might have usually meant that he was not accepted in the highest circles of society, John seems to have had a reputation as a "man of culture" who invited artists and thinkers to his home. It was there he met Mary Robinson, and they struck up a friendship. Mary always downplayed their connection, but John kept many of the letters that they exchanged and embellished on them when he published *Letters from Perdita to a Certain Israelite* in 1781.

In 1798 Charlotte and Sophia published their first joint work, *Trifles of Helicon*, a book of poetry they dedicated to their father. The dedication was somewhat tongue in cheek, as John had recently declared bankruptcy and the sisters wanted to prove that the money he had spent on their education had been worth it.

Like her father's, Charlotte's own romantic relationships were complicated. She had three children with Nicholas Byrne, editor of the *Morning Post*, before they finally married in 1815. Charlotte also worked for Nicholas, writing poetry under the pseudonym Rosa Matilda.

Charlotte published her most famous work, *Zofloya; or, The Moor: A Romance of the Fifteenth Century*, in 1806. It is a Gothic novel unlike many of its contemporaries. Charlotte's heroine Victoria is a sadistic murderer whose journey more closely follows that of a Gothic hero. Victoria's sexual knowledge and appetite for pleasure led to moral objections to Charlotte's work in many reviews. Indeed, Victoria's downfall comes from her partnership with Zofloya, and Charlotte shows us the dark side of marriage for women when they lose their identity and financial independence.

Charlotte's style is comparable to her contemporary Mary Shelley, the author of *Frankenstein*. Mary's husband, Percy Shelley, was a fan of Charlotte's, but the couple's friend Byron was not. He referenced Charlotte, using her pen name Rosa, in his satirical poem *English Bards and Scotch Reviewers* (1809)—which he wrote after his first book of poems received a brutal review in the *Edinburgh Review*. In the poem he mocks the leading writers of Romanticism.

Far be't from me unkindly to upbraid
The lovely Rosa's prose in masquerade,
Whose strains, the faithful echoes of her mind,
Leave wondering comprehension far behind.[10]

Meanwhile, Sophia was publishing her own novels. The first, an anti-Jacobin novel, *Waldorf; or the dangers of Philosophy*, appeared in 1798. She published five more novels during her life.

The sisters, and their novels, are unique. They don't fit into the larger theme of Jewish women working to make themselves and their religion more palatable through careful outreach and education. The King sisters refused, in both their personal lives and their work, to toe the line. They resist categorization. They're a fascinating, compelling example of Jewish women writers in the early nineteenth century.

CONCLUSION

One traditional line of Jewish history traces modern Jewish culture from the Berlin Haskalah (Enlightenment) in the early eighteenth century. Tradition goes that, for the first time, German Jews of the time began to look outside their own insular academic and social circles with a purpose of assimilating and participating more fully in the Christian and secular worlds.

This history is at odds with the history of the Jews in England, especially wealthy Sephardim, who began to assimilate and modernize upon their arrival in England.

And here we can see one of the major difficulties in discussing religion and popular attitudes toward practitioners of a religion. Extant sources can only give us a part of the picture. If we learn anything from the brilliant and complicated Jewish women of the nineteenth century it should be that they existed in this space between acceptance and anti-Semitism. It is not an either-or. They lived with this question every day, and in every way. Their art and lives can only be considered in that context.

As Todd Endelman writes, "They were willing, often eager, to exchange some or many of the values and institutions of traditional Jewish life for the dominant mores of the states in which they lived, either because they believed that such values were necessary for survival or success in the modern world, or because they were convinced that these mores represented a genuinely superior cultural system."[11]

It is easy to divest ourselves from theoretical questions like these, but the Jewish women of the nineteenth century lived them every day. Each woman profiled in this chapter chose, over and over, to engage with her Christian and secular counterparts, with an eye to assimilating and educating. "The Jew" as depicted in nineteenth-century caricatures and fiction was very real and harmful to these women and their way of life. They chose to actively fight against these stereotypes in myriad ways, even going so far as to challenge the artists spreading them. They were not passive viewers of cultural norms; they took every opportunity and venue available to them to spread the truth about their Judaism.

Recommended Reading

Abrams, Nita. The Courier Series. Zebra Romance, 2002.

Ashton, Dianne. *Rebecca Gratz: Women and Judaism in Antebellum America.* Wayne State University Press, 1997.

Cherry, Deborah. *Painting Women: Victorian Women Artists.* Routledge, 1993.

Dacre, Charlotte. *Zofloya; or, The Moor: A Romance of the Fifteenth Century.* Edited by Adriana Cracium. Broadview Literary Texts, 1997.

Daniels, Jeffery. *Solomon: A Family of Painters.* Exhibition catalog. Geffrye Museum and Birmingham Museum & Art Gallery, 1986.

Endelman, Todd M. *The Jews of Georgian England 1714–1830.* University of Michigan Press, 1999.

Goodman, Susan, editor. *The Emergence of Jewish Artists in Nineteenth-Century Europe.* Exhibition catalog. Merrell and Jewish Museum, 2001.

Jones, Ann. *Ideas and Innovations: Best Sellers of Jane Austen's Age.* AMS Press, 1986.

Lerner, Rose. *True Pretenses.* 2015.

Tierney, Suzanne. *The Art of the Scandal.* 2018.

Wilson, Lisa. "Female Pseudonymity in the Romantic 'Age of Personality': The Career of Charlotte King/Rosa Matilda/Charlotte Dacre." *European Romantic Review* 9, no. 3 (1998).

CONCLUSION

Our Regency

Ten short years in the grand scheme of history.

But a singular moment. A clearly inimitable period, distinct from the eras around it in subtle but important ways that have led to an enduring fascination.

Why? Everyone wants to know. What about the Regency continues to draw us in?

I wish I had the answer (I would make millions of dollars).

I hope what is clear is that there is a duality here: The Regency was a unique moment, and that uniqueness has inspired everything that has come after, and those two Regencies—the real one and the fictionalized one—have melded and brought us to where we are today.

The Regency is a period of fascination for so many—academics, novelists, filmmakers, casual readers, and amateur history enthusiasts alike fall for its charms. And so we are given many versions of the Regency, overlaid with each individual's biases and affections.

We have a tendency to stereotype historical eras. The Regency's stereotype is born from beloved fiction both historical and contemporary—and to ignore this pastiche is to miss something essential to the Regency era we know today. The world Jane Austen created, and so many imitated after, is so real we feel like we are just a step away as a reader.

Like so many, I have a deeply personal relationship with the Regency due to the hundreds of romance novels I have read set in the period. The ballrooms of Almack's and the country manors of earls and dukes were brought to life for me from a very specific perspective: that of a romance heroine.

Regency romance novels center on women. Their sexual desires, of course. But also their ambitions. Their triumphs and their failures. Their friendships and their relationships. Regency romance novels told me that there have always been ambitious and passionate women throughout history; we just need to look for them.

Regency romance novels challenged me to consider the real history from the perspective of the young fictional women I was reading about. These novels are peppered with historical events ranging from the comet of 1812 to the Napoleonic Wars, and the heroines interact and react to these events, encouraging the reader to consider the interior and emotional lives of women—a facet often missing from history books.

Regency romance novels get knocked for historical inaccuracy all the time. Critics say that their historical setting is simply window dressing. But that's not true at all. Regency romance novelists do their homework. Their works often include bibliographies or author's notes where the reader is brought into the creative process, getting a peek at what actual historical figure, event, text, image, what have you, inspired the author.

So many of the women profiled in this book put pen to page and left behind a written record. In letters, journals, novels, poems, plays, and memoirs the women of the Regency wrote themselves into the historical narrative.

In the way of history, many of these women have been forgotten or reduced to single sentences. Networks of women have been fractured, with some lucky women separated out and held up as trailblazers, making it difficult to connect the original circles. But whether connected in real life or later by historians, these webs of women spread across the entire Regency era.

"Boldly mould, invent, design,"[1] Georgiana, Duchess of Devonshire, urged her niece Lady Caroline Lamb in her Christmas poem.

Those words echo through time, particularly poignant to a modern reader who can see what history has done to these vibrant, complicated women.

They remind us of the human side of these networks—the real relationships at the heart of these webs—and the resilience of women's words. Georgiana, Caroline, and so many others left us their words. They wrote their own stories. They were mad and bad and dangerous to know.

ACKNOWLEDGMENTS

An author gets to put her name on the cover of a book but an enormous number of people help bring that idea of a book into a reality, and I will do my best to thank everyone who has helped this one come into existence. If I have forgotten anyone, I am so sorry from the bottom of my heart.

First thanks go to my editor, Maddie Caldwell. She believed in my idea and helped make it so much better and so much more book-like. I am grateful for her patience, thoughtfulness, and generosity during this process. Many thanks also to Jacqui Young, who helped so much with image permissions and more. And thank you to Liz Connor who designed the beautiful, perfect cover for this book—you realized the spirit of this book exactly.

Second thanks to my agent, Holly Root. I couldn't ask for a better partner and guide through the book-writing world.

Third, I need to thank my family for so much I barely know where to start. Thank you to my dad, Steve, who takes every single phone call, no matter the time of day or what he's doing, and then gives the best advice about what to do; to my brother, Jacob, who gives me such love and support and the gift of the best sister-in-law in the world, Olivia. To Olivia, the sister I've gained, the person I turn to whenever I need a boost of confidence, and writing advice—our family is so lucky to have you. And Mo, as I'm writing this, I haven't met you yet but you're coming so soon and I know you're going to be the best nephew ever. Finally to Leah, my sister, my business partner, my best friend, the person who is always there and who I will always be there for, I do not deserve you.

A million thanks as well to my extended family of Cohns, Connors, Doctoroffs, Donnellys, Duboises, Kochs, Liebmans, Milches, and Tuckers. I am so lucky to have a family that always shows up for each other.

Like my family, my friends deserve too many thanks to put here, but I will try. Rebekah and Sarah, who have shared so much life and writing advice on so many couches, and so many episodes of *Love Island*, I'm so lucky to have such generous and brilliant writers who are also amazing friends. Lizzy, who has been my biggest cheerleader forever, and both Emmas, and Louisa, thank you for your support for so many years. Miranda and Lily, so much has changed since college but your friendship and love remain a constant that I'll always be grateful for. Emma Straub, you are such a generous friend and guide through our extremely bizarre, specific intersection of life—thank you.

I started dating someone a few months before my book was due, which I would not recommend. But Blake, you were so worth it. You've taught me that things happen at exactly the moment they are meant to. Thank you for your unbelievable support, patience, and understanding during this process. I love you more than I can really say.

NOTES

Introduction to the Regency World and Why We're Here

1. S. Morgan, *Lady Morgan's Memoirs* (Allen and Co., vol. 2, 1863), 200.
2. P. Douglass, *Lady Caroline Lamb: A Biography* (Palgrave Macmillan, 2016), 5.

Chapter One: The Ton: Either You're In or You're Out

1. This upper class was generally referred to as the Ton, short for *le bon ton*, French for "in the fashionable mode."
2. Jane Rendell, *The Pursuit of Pleasure: Gender, Space, and Architecture in Regency England* (Rutgers University Press, 2002).
3. Henry Luttrell, *Advice to Julia* (John Murray, 1820), 11–12.
4. R. Gronow, *Reminiscences of Captain Gronow* (Smith and Elder, 1862).
5. Dorothea Lieven and Lionel G. Robinson, *Letters of Dorothea, Princess Lieven, During Her Residence in London, 1812–1834* (Longmans, Green, 1902).
6. Lieven and Robinson, *Letters of Dorothea, Princess Lieven*, 29.
7. Lieven and Robinson, *Letters of Dorothea, Princess Lieven*, 48.
8. J. Kloester, *Georgette Heyer's Regency World* (Sourcebooks, 2010), 89.
9. E. Beresford Chancellor, *Memorials of St. James's Street, Together with the Annals of Almack's* (G. Richards, 1922).
10. Henry Greville, *Leaves from the Diary of Henry Greville* (Smith and Elder, 4th edition, 1905), 309.
11. Greville, *Leaves from the Diary of Henry Greville*, 310.
12. Sarah Knowles Bolton, *Famous English Statesmen of Queen Victoria's Reign* (T. Y. Crowell, 1891), 85.

13. *The Times*, May 23, 1834: 5.
14. Judith Lissauer Cromwell, *Dorothea Lieven: A Russian Princess in London and Paris, 1785–1857* (McFarland, 2007), 251.
15. G. Heyer, *Friday's Child* (Arrow Books, 2019).
16. Gronow, *Reminiscences of Captain Gronow.*
17. Lieven and Robinson. *Letters of Dorothea, Princess Lieven.*
18. T. Londonderry, *Robert Stewart, Viscount Castlereagh* (Arthur L. Humphreys, 1902), 15.

Chapter Two: Game of Thrones

1. *The Gentleman's and London Magazine: and Monthly Chronologer* 30, 1761.
2. E. Holt, *The Public and Domestic Life of George the Third*, vol. 1 (Sherwood, Neely, and Jones, 1820), 26.
3. Holt, *The Public and Domestic Life of George the Third*, 493.
4. Holt, *The Public and Domestic Life of George the Third*, 609.
5. P. Fitzgerald, *The Life of George the Fourth*, vol. 1 (Tinsley Brothers, 1881), 279.
6. Jane Robins, *Rebel Queen: The Trial of Queen Caroline* (Simon and Schuster, 2006), 16.
7. Robins, *Rebel Queen*, 16.
8. *Jane Austen's Letters*, ed. D. Le Faye (University of Oxford Press, 2011), 208.
9. Flora Fraser, *The Unruly Queen: The Life of Queen Caroline* (Bloomsbury, 1996), 266.
10. J. Van der Kiste, *Georgian Princess* (Sutton Publishing, 2000).
11. Robins, *Rebel Queen*, 313.
12. Robins, *Rebel Queen*, 313.
13. James Chambers, *Charlotte & Leopold: The True Romance of the Prince Regent's Daughter* (Old Street, 2008), 3.
14. K. Williams, *Becoming Queen Victoria* (Ballantine Books, 2008), 50.
15. Williams, *Becoming Queen Victoria*, 64.
16. Williams, *Becoming Queen Victoria*, 64.

17. A. Plowden, *Caroline and Charlotte: Regency Scandals* (History Press, 2011).
18. Plowden, *Caroline and Charlotte.*
19. Lieven and Robinson. *Letters of Dorothea, Princess Lieven.*
20. Chambers, *Charlotte & Leopold*, 169.
21. Robins, *Rebel Queen*, 51.
22. Chambers, *Charlotte & Leopold*, 187.
23. Plowden, *Caroline and Charlotte.*
24. Williams, *Becoming Queen Victoria*, 137.
25. Chambers, *Charlotte & Leopold*, 199.
26. Chambers, *Charlotte & Leopold*, 228.
27. "A Definitive History of Prince Harry and Meghan Markle's Royal Relationship," *Town & Country*, May 8, 2019.

Chapter Three: Mistresses

1. A. Stott, *Hannah More: The First Victorian* (Oxford University Press, 2003), 10.
2. D. Robinson, "*The Duchess*, Mary Robinson, and Georgiana's Social Network," *Wordsworth Circle* 42, no. 3 (2011): 193.
3. M. Robinson, *Memoirs of the Late Mrs. Robinson, Written by Herself*, 4 vols. (R. Phillips, 1801), 93.
4. Robinson, *Memoirs of the Late Mrs. Robinson*, 102.
5. Paula Byrne and Diana Bishop, *Perdita: The Life of Mary Robinson* (ISIS, 2009), 101.
6. Byrne and Bishop, *Perdita*, 118.
7. Joel Haefner, "(De)Forming the Romantic Canon: The Case of Women Writers," *College Literature* 20, no. 2 (June 1993): 44.
8. Byrne and Bishop, *Perdita*, 392.
9. *Town and Country*, 1774.
10. Jo Manning, *My Lady Scandalous: The Amazing Life and Outrageous Times of Grace Dalrymple Elliott, Royal Courtesan* (Simon and Schuster, 2005), 96.
11. *Morning Herald*, December 24, 1781.

12. G. Elliott, *Journal of My Life During the French Revolution* (Richard Bentley, 1859), 137.
13. Melinda Graefe, "'Dido, in Despair!' Emma Hamilton's Attitudes and the Shape of Mourning in *Persuasion*," *JASNA* 38 no. 3 (Summer 2018).
14. P. Douglass, *Lady Caroline Lamb: A Biography* (Palgrave Macmillan, 2016), 35.
15. Morgan, *Lady Morgan's Memoirs*, 200. (Allen and Co, vol. 2, 1863).
16. Douglass, *Lady Caroline Lamb*, 100.
17. Douglass, *Lady Caroline Lamb*, 102.
18. G. Byron and Leslie Marchand, *Byron's Letters and Journals*, vol. 2 (Belknap Press, 1973), 170–71.
19. Byron and Marchand, *Byron's Letters and Journals*, vol. 2, 260.
20. Douglass, *Lady Caroline Lamb*, 125.
21. Douglass, *Lady Caroline Lamb*, 167.
22. Douglass, *Lady Caroline Lamb*, 184.
23. C. Lamb, *Glenarvon*, 3rd ed. (Colburn, 1816).
24. Lamb, *Glenarvon*, 536.
25. A. Larman, *Byron's Women* (Head of Zeus, 2018).
26. Douglass, *Lady Caroline Lamb*, 193.
27. M. Airlie, *Lady Palmerston and Her Times*, vol. 2 (Hodder and Stoughton, 1922), 39.
28. "Biography: Lady Caroline Lamb," *Literary Gazette*, 1828: 107–08.
29. Mary Robinson, *A Letter to the Women of England and The Natural Daughter*, ed. Sharon Setzer (Broadview Literary Texts, 2003), 47.

Chapter Four: The Family Business: Artistic Families

1. Diane Waggoner, *The Sharples Collection: A Brief Introduction to the Microfilm Edition of the Sharples Family Collection* (Microform Academic, 2001), 6.
2. Waggoner, *The Sharples Collection*, 18.
3. Waggoner, *The Sharples Collection*, 17.
4. Waggoner, *The Sharples Collection*, 18.
5. J. Hanes, "Shady Ladies: Female Silhouette Artists of the 18th Century," *Antiques Journal*, June 2009: 27.

6. She published *Dangers of Coquetry* in 1790 when she was just eighteen, but it was published anonymously.
7. R. Manvell, *Sarah Siddons: Life of an Actress* (Putnam, 1970), 96.
8. George Byron, ed. Thomas Moore. *Letters and Journals of Lord Byron* (J. and J. Harper, 1830), 460.
9. Catherine Clinton, *Fanny Kemble's Civil Wars* (Oxford University Press, 2001), 37.
10. F. Kemble, *Journal of a Residence on a Georgian Plantation in 1838–1839* (Harper and Brothers, 1864), 199.
11. P. Butler, *Mr. Butler's Statement* (J. C. Clark, 1850), 9.

Chapter Five: Our STEM Foremothers

1. Caroline Lucretia Herschel, *Memoir and Correspondence of Caroline Herschel* (Murray, 1876).
2. Herschel, *Memoir and Correspondence of Caroline Herschel.*
3. Herschel, *Memoir and Correspondence of Caroline Herschel.*
4. Herschel, *Memoir and Correspondence of Caroline Herschel.*
5. Herschel, *Memoir and Correspondence of Caroline Herschel.*
6. Emily Winterburn. "Learned Modesty and the First Lady's Comet: A Commentary on Caroline Herschel (1787) 'An Account of a New Comet,'" *Royal Society Philosophical Transactions A* 373, no. 2039 (April 13, 2015).
7. "Mrs. Somerville Obituary," *Morning Post*, December 2, 1872.
8. M. Somerville, *Personal Recollections, from Early Life to Old Age, of Mary Somerville: With Selections from Her Correspondence* (Roberts Brothers, 1874, digitized 2007, original in Harvard University), 28.
9. Richard Holmes, "The Royal Society's Lost Women Scientists," *Guardian*, November 20, 2010, www.theguardian.com/science/2010/nov/21/royal-society-lost-women-scientists.
10. Charlotte Still, "Jane Marcet: 175 Faces of Chemistry," 2014, www.rsc.org/diversity/175-faces/all-faces/jane-marcet.

11. Mary T. Brück, *Women in Early British and Irish Astronomy: Stars and Satellites* (Springer, 2009), 64.
12. Shelley Emling, *The Fossil Hunter: Dinosaurs, Evolution, and the Woman Whose Discoveries Changed the World* (Palgrave Macmillan, 2011), 55.
13. Emling, *The Fossil Hunter*, 65.
14. "Mary Anning (1799–1847)," Geological Society, www.geolsoc.org.uk/Library-and-Information-Services/Exhibitions/Women-and-Geology/Mary-Anning.
15. "Mary Buckland Née Morland (1797–1857)," Geological Society, www.geolsoc.org.uk/Library-and-Information-Services/Exhibitions/Women-and-Geology/Mary-Buckland.
16. C. V. Burek and B. Higgs, *The Role of Women in the History of Geology* (Geological Society, 2007).
17. Emling, *The Fossil Hunter*, 157.

Chapter Six: The Fairer Sex

1. Jonathan David Gross, *The Life of Anne Damer: Portrait of a Regency Artist* (Lexington Books, 2014), 34.
2. There is no evidence of a physical relationship, and therefore historians have been reluctant to name Anne and Mary's relationship as a lesbian relationship. This is an issue scholars of the LGBTQ community often face when trying to "prove" a historical figure's sexuality.
3. Anne Lister, Diaries, 1821.
4. Anne Lister, Diaries, 1823.
5. Elizabeth Mavor, *The Ladies of Llangollen: A Study of Romantic Friendship* (Moonrise Press, 2011).
6. Susan Vallardes, "An Introduction to the Literary Persons of Anne Lister and the Ladies of Llangollen," *Literature Compass*, April 2013.
7. Anne Lister and Helena Whitbread, *I Know My Own Heart: The Diaries of Anne Lister, 1791–1840* (New York University Press, 1992), 200.

Chapter Seven: Historical Accuracy and Regency England

1. Paula Byrne, *Belle* (W. F. Howes, 2014).
2. Byrne, *Belle*.
3. Gretchen Gerzina, *Black London: Life Before Emancipation* (Rutgers University Press, 1995), 88–89.
4. *Belle* (film directed by Amma Asante, 2013).
5. Kevin Rawlinson, "Another Gove U-Turn: Mary Seacole Will Remain on the Curriculum," *Independent*, 2013, www.independent.co.uk/news/uk/politics/another-gove-u-turn-mary-seacole-will-remain-on-the-curriculum-8485472.html.
6. Mary Seacole, *Wonderful Adventures of Mrs Seacole in Many Lands* (Dover Publications, 2019), chapter 1.
7. Seacole, *Wonderful Adventures of Mrs Seacole in Many Lands*, chapter 1.
8. Seacole, *Wonderful Adventures of Mrs Seacole in Many Lands*, chapter 4.
9. Seacole, *Wonderful Adventures of Mrs Seacole in Many Lands*, chapter 8.
10. Seacole, *Wonderful Adventures of Mrs Seacole in Many Lands*, chapter 8.
11. Bidisha, "Tudor, English and Black—and Not a Slave in Sight," *Guardian*, 2017, www.theguardian.com/world/2017/oct/29/tudor-english-black-not-slave-in-sight-miranda-kaufmann-history.

Chapter Eight: Educators and Ambassadors: Jewish Women in the Regency

1. *Kentish Gazette*, April 21, 1809.
2. A Lady. *The Jewish Manual: or, Practical Information in Jewish and Modern Cookery, with a Collection of Valuable Recipes & Hints Relating to the Toilette* (T. & W. Boone, 1846).
3. Rollin G. Osterweis, *Rebecca Gratz: A Study in Charm* (Putnam, 1935), 151.
4. Rachel Mordecai Lazarus et al., *The Education of the Heart: The Correspondence of Rachel Mordecai Lazarus and Maria Edgeworth* (University of North Carolina Press, 2012), 16–17.

5. Honora Sneyd is such a fascinating figure and worthy of her own book entirely. She was raised with the poet Anna Seward, and the pair shared an intense friendship that historians continue to debate about to this day. The poems Anna wrote for Honora are passionate and intense, and they're frequently included in discussions of female friendships and lesbianism.
6. Lazarus, *The Education of the Heart*.
7. Lazarus, *The Education of the Heart*.
8. Beth-Zion Lack Abrahams, *Grace Aguilar: A Centenary Tribute*, vol. 16 (Jewish Historical Society of England), 140.
9. Abrahams, *Grace Aguilar*, 140.
10. G. Byron, *English Bards and Scotch Reviewers* (James Cawthorn, 1809).
11. Todd M. Endelman, *The Jews of Georgian England: 1714–1830: Tradition and Change in a Liberal Society* (University of Michigan Press, 1999).

Conclusion: Our Regency

1. P. Douglass, *Lady Caroline Lamb: a Biography* (Palgrave Macmillan, 2016), 4.

INDEX

ABOUT THE AUTHOR

Debut author **Bea Koch** is one of the owners of the Ripped Bodice, an independent bookstore in the United States dedicated to romance. In addition to being a groundbreaking bookseller, Bea graduated from Yale with distinction as the last Renaissance Studies major and received an MA from NYU: Steinhardt in Costume History. She is the proud mother of dog Fitzwilliam Waffles. He has more followers on Instagram than she does.